When God performs a ⟨...⟩ in you—one that even no⟨...⟩ you want to tell the world. Sue Wynn has done just that. Speaking from the heart and by the Holy Spirit, she retells a frightening part of her life that reveals the glory of the Lord and will change the reader's life.

—MARK ALAN LESLIE
AUTHOR, MIDNIGHT RIDER FOR THE MORNING STAR

The bottom line: the Spirit of God graces Sue with healing—both spiritual and physical. One reads this book in awe and can only say, to God alone goes glory, or to put it in classical format: *soli deo gloria.*

—DR. DONALD DEMARAY
PROFESSOR EMERITUS, ASBURY THEOLOGICAL SEMINARY

Sue Wynn's story is a modern day miraculous fulfillment of Psalm 107:20: "He sent forth His word and healed them."

—ALETHA HINTHORN, AUTHOR
DIRECTOR, COME TO THE FIRE MINISTRIES
FOUNDER, WOMEN ALIVE
KANSAS CITY, MISSOURI

*From Death to Life* leaves you wanting to read more about this Christian walk of faith. This book is a true testimony of a disciple of Christ who chose to believe that God's Word means what it says, even today. Tormented for years by an incurable disease, Sue Wynn decided to cry out to God, challenging His Word. A glorious read.

—DAVID UBER
PASTOR, TEACHER, AND DISCIPLE OF CHRIST

# FROM DEATH TO LIFE

*Michael —*
*May this bless you!*

## SUSAN WYNN

CREATION
**HOUSE**

From Death to Life by Susan Wynn
Published by Creation House
A Charisma Media Company
600 Rinehart Road
Lake Mary, Florida 32746
www.charismamedia.com

Unless otherwise noted, all Scripture quotations are from the New American Standard Bible—Updated Edition, Copyright © 1960, 1962, 1963, 1968, 1971, 1972, 1973, 1975, 1977, 1995 by The Lockman Foundation. Used by permission. (www.Lockman.org)

Scripture quotations marked AMP are from the Amplified Bible. Old Testament copyright © 1965, 1987 by the Zondervan Corporation. The Amplified New Testament copyright © 1954, 1958, 1987 by the Lockman Foundation. Used by permission.

Scripture quotations marked KJV are from the King James Version of the Bible.

Scripture quotations marked NIV are from the Holy Bible, New International Version of the Bible. Copyright © 1973, 1978, 1984, International Bible Society. Used by permission.

Design Director: Bill Johnson
Cover design by Nathan Morgan
Cover image courtesy of Sherwood A. Burton and Reid State Park, Maine; author photo courtesy of Ron Tucker

Visit the author's website: www.susanwynnwords.com, and blog: fromdeathtolife.wordpress.com

Library of Congress Cataloging-in-Publication Data: 2011943894
International Standard Book Number: 978-1-61638-828-7
E-book International Standard Book Number: 978-1-61638-829-4

While the author has made every effort to provide accurate telephone numbers and Internet addresses at the time of publication, neither the publisher nor the author assumes any responsibility for errors or for changes that occur after publication.

First edition

11 12 13 14 15 — 987654321
Printed in Canada

# ACKNOWLEDGMENTS

THE TRIUNE GOD—How can I thank You, Lord, for giving me a glorious testimony of Your work in my life? Only by shouting from the rooftops what You whispered in my ear; so here goes, Lord Jesus! If You are glorified, God, I am satisfied.

Dr. Donald Demaray—My book was lifeless until you opened a well of creativity in me. Thank you for your kindness to a "raw" author!

Mark Alan Leslie—An editor, indeed! Thank you for your friendship and fellowship in the Lord. I pray the Lord will profusely bless Loy and you, both here and in heaven.

David "Doc" Uber—Your obedience to the Lord set me free from my captivity and prepared the way for me to enter life as God has it. May the Lord Jesus bless you, indeed, for your faithfulness to hear and obey the Spirit's lead.

My dear husband, Jeff—You walked with me through the nightmare of MS and into the marvelous light of Christ! We are one, joined at the heart by Jesus Christ. What a joy it is to be married to you and to minister to Christ and His people with you.

My brothers and sisters in Christ...How many of you have walked beside me on my journey with Jesus? It's beyond my ability to reckon. I know that your encouragement, exhortation, prayers, and ears to hear the Spirit will be remembered when you stand before Jesus.

# TABLE OF CONTENTS

# FOREWORD

**T**HIS IS GOD!" exclaimed the neurologist. He had just witnessed a miracle. No more tremors; better, not a single sign of MS.

But that's impossible, declared the local newspaper editor. We can't publish that story.

Yet doctors documented the healing. And other healings came too: carpal tunnel, allergies, asthma.

It all began with reconciliation. Reconciliation between Sue and God, followed by forgiveness of people who had done her dirt. Then comes the healing. Listen to Susan Wynn's own words:

"...I rise from my couch to go to bed. Strength comes through my whole body! I lie in bed, overwhelmed with joy...."

And to cap the climax: "Morning arrives. Fatigue is no longer my companion."

The bottom line: the Spirit of God graces Sue with healing—both spiritual and physical.

Husband Jeff, seeing the clear evidence of his changed wife, comes to know God as Savior. Today both engage in Christian ministry. They do it together, working as evangelists and ministering restoration and empowerment to hurting pastors. Ministry includes gospel proclamation with worship, Bible study and therapy.

Therapy—you guessed it, both spiritual and physical healing.

One reads this book in awe and can only say, to God alone goes glory, or to put it in classical format: *soli deo gloria.*

—DR. DONALD E. DEMARAY
PROFESSOR EMERITUS, ASBURY THEOLOGICAL SEMINARY

# Chapter One

# ENTER MY NIGHTMARE

THE LA-Z-BOY IS my oasis, soft and familiar in my suddenly hard and strange world. I wearily sink down into it. Finally, my jerking head and knotted muscles find some respite. Pots and dishes clatter in the kitchen as Jeff prepares spaghetti for dinner. I breathe in the fragrant, comforting aroma. In moments I fall asleep.

"Hey, hon, dinner's ready!"

I hear Jeff's voice but I can't wake up! Death has me in its grip. It doesn't want to let go. I'm paralyzed, unable to take a breath. Part of me wants to give up and die so I won't have to deal with this hard life anymore.

"Don't give up! Breathe!" my brain screams.

My heart racing from fear, I struggle, take a deep breath and wake up to life turned upside down. Violent tremors shake my head, neck, and right shoulder. Fatigue, perpetual pain, and paralysis have joined them as my new companions. The doctors say, "Nursing home in five years? Probably so."

Plans and dreams? They've evaporated like a morning mist in the harsh light of my new reality.

Enter my nightmare. I don't recognize my life anymore. Stop! Police! I've been robbed! Job? Money? Bright future? All have vanished. Smart, organized, fit, clever, and innovative Sue? Hijacked to who-knows-where. I don't know who did it, officer. I couldn't see his face.

I'm the perfect poster girl for multiple sclerosis (MS). What an honor! The MS Society asks me to be on their speaker's bureau. Yeah, I'll stand up before all of their corporate sponsors and potential donors, shaking from head to toe, and say, "Life is hell with MS, but I'm going to be strong."

The corporate folks are deeply touched when I speak. They give much money to the cause. Let's get some research going, and wipe out MS.

Meanwhile, MS snickers in the corner. *Research all you want. I'm incurable. I attack a part of the body that puzzles clinical types. Besides, you know almost nothing about me and my Little Helpers.*

That's my opponent, MS. Its Little Helpers used to be my friends, fighting off disease in my body. Now they're eating the insulation on the nerves in my brain and spinal cord. In their eyes, it's enemy tissue. On a search-and-destroy mission, they gobble with great gusto. My body short-circuits.

I'm in a life-and-death prizefight. Research tells me that after a long and ugly battle, I'll die early from the damage MS inflicts on my brain and spinal cord. Why not just give up? Not this girl. I'm a fighter.

I flail angrily at MS. With all the bravado I can muster, I yell, "I'm going to beat you!" It strikes back ten times as hard. I fall down. The round ends and I struggle back to my corner. My trainer frantically fans a towel at me, trying to revive me so I can go another round with it.

"Here, take a drink of water," he says. I choke it down.

The bell sounds. I lurch from the stool and stagger back out into the ring. MS is a lot bigger than me. This isn't a fair fight.

The "clinicals" look at me like some kind of challenge rather than a hurting human being. Here's a tough case. Let's do this test, and even though that one is painful, maybe we'll learn some more.

I undergo endless testing with no relief in sight. I stagger from one clinical to another. All of them spout clinical jargon, poking and prodding me, then scratching their heads. They want to help but there's very little they can do.

MS says, *Gotcha!*

The Little Helpers are dazzled at the smorgasbord as they enter my brain through the gaping hole MS punches in my blood-brain barrier. Nobody knows how that happens.

*If we munch over here, her legs go into continual charley-horse mode,* they say. *If we chew over there, her bladder perpetually and painfully spasms. Oh, look over here at the optic nerves! They look like they'd be especially tasty as an evening snack.*

Zap! Now my vision is distorted, like I'm looking at the world through a kaleidoscope.

It isn't fair. It's a dirty trick. Jeff and I are living the American Dream. This can't be happening. Only forty, I'm happily married and about to receive a promotion to executive management. Life couldn't be better. Surprise!

A couple of years before my nightmare begins, I remember God. I haven't seen Him for a long time, not since Sunday school. Even then He was only a faint image. Maybe I can visit Him in church. I'll ask Jeff what he thinks.

Jeff's expression speaks louder than words. He doesn't believe in God.

We agree that people in church are hypocrites, saying one thing and doing another. Let's not examine our own lives, though. That would be uncomfortable.

I guess I won't check out God after all. The empty place remains. Filling it was just a passing thought.

What is God, anyway? I've fashioned my own god, of one part Buddhism, one part Hinduism, one part New Age, one part of something I call "the lord" and a dash of my version of Jesus. I decide Jesus came in all kinds of ways to all kinds of cultures. That sounds good. They're all really Jesus, just dressed differently. If someone asks me whether I'm a Christian, though, I'm quick to say yes.

In the MS corner of the ring, the trainer appears. He's the man downstairs.

*That's good, Sue,* he says. *Stay away from God. You don't need Jesus, anyway. You're a good person.*

Then, so softly I can't quite hear it, he sneers, *When you die you can come to my place. Do you think you're in hell now? I'll welcome you with open arms to the real deal.*

## A PREVIEW OF COMING ATTRACTIONS

In my late twenties I experience a preview of coming attractions. MS makes its first appearance on the stage of my life.

*Ta-da! Here I am, you lucky girl. My Little Helpers are going to start by chewing a bit on your optic nerves.*

My eyes in kaleidoscope mode, Jeff and I scurry to the ER. I enter the clinical scene. The territory is unfamiliar and terrifying.

The clinicals say, "Let's test your eyes. Hmm. You can't see all parts of the letters on the eye chart? You can't see all the fingers on your hands? What you see looks like hash instead of steak? You have optic neuritis. Your optic nerve is inflamed, but we don't know why. You need to see your eye doctor tomorrow."

What just hit me? The punch came out of nowhere.

MS says, *Be very subtle, Little Helpers. I don't want anyone to know who we are yet. Let's just make her suffer off and on for now. Later, we'll ruin her life entirely.*

My eye doctor carefully and silently examines my eyes. I hold my breath.

He says, "Your optic nerves are inflamed. I'm not sure, but it could be that some kind of virus is attacking them. Let's see if your vision improves over the next couple of days. If it doesn't, come back again."

A virus, you say? That sounds good to me. It will eventually die off, and I'll be able to see again. My vision improves. It must have been a virus.

Time passes. My vision changes to kaleidoscope mode again, and I return to the stark light of the ER. The clinical says in typical clinical jargon, "Do you know that these repeated episodes of optic neuritis indicate that you have a 50 percent chance of having multiple sclerosis?"

Not me. MS is out of the question. I'm busy with life and I don't have time for MS. Sorry.

"Ladies and gentlemen," cries the referee. "Welcome to tonight's boxing match. In this corner, Susan Dumbfounded Wynn. And in this corner, MS and its Little Helpers!"

One day while I'm out in the garden, my legs turn to rubber. MS delivers a kidney punch. I wobble, barely making it back to the stool in my corner of the ring. I look around blindly. Who hit me?

I rest in the coolness of the house. Still weak and shaky, I decide eating something might help. I feel better after my snack. Maybe my sugar was low. I return to my beloved garden.

MS says, *That's really good, Sue. Keep thinking it's something easy to treat. Low blood sugar is a great idea. Me and my little friends want to remain anonymous for now.*

The Little Helpers said, *Yum! That was an especially tasty bit of spinal cord sheath. What an audacious appetizer! C'mon everyone! It's time for the main course. How delectable! Let's chew on a spot she won't notice for a long time.*

# Chapter Two

# THE NIGHTMARE BEGINS

THE BIG DAY arrives. It's April 12, 1996. The Little Helpers have munched on my brain and spinal cord for years.

*It's time to give Sue and Jeff a taste of hell*, MS says, popping me in the nose again and again.

A normal day turns crazy when my head suddenly begins to bob uncontrollably.

"What's going on?" I say with just a hint of terror in my voice.

We rush to the ER once again. Jeff is worried that I might be having a stroke. I'm just plain scared.

The ER clinical says, "It's not a stroke." We breathe a sigh of relief.

"We'll run some blood tests," he says. "You might have hypercalcemia, too much calcium in your blood. That can cause tremors."

The test results are normal.

I ask, "But what's causing the tremor?"

"I don't know," the ER clinical says, "but see your regular doctor tomorrow. Though not emergent, I believe your condition is very serious."

Sleepless night, anyone? Sure, why not? Jeff and I worry the night away, imagining what might be wrong with me.

The next day, I visit Nice-doctor, scared out of my wits.

She says, "You've been my patient for years. I've been monitoring you carefully. You've had multiple episodes of optic neuritis and muscle weakness. I think this is MS."

That's what my neighbor had. She died in a fetal position. Aunt Dot has MS, too. She walks on the sides of her twisted feet and uses a walker. It takes her a long time to climb just a couple of stairs, but she's still sharp, still hanging in there.

More clinical words come from Nice-doctor, even some tears. She's a good one.  My mind swims as I hear, "Sending you to a neurologist, treatment right away, maybe inpatient stay, IV therapy." Yesterday was normal. Now I feel like I've entered the Twilight Zone.

Back at our home, I try to pack my suitcase in preparation for the potential hospital stay. I have no idea what I'm doing. I can't even decide on which pajamas to bring. Jeff takes over, thank goodness. Tears stand in his eyes as he packs my things.

## ENTER ULTRA-CLINICAL

Jeff and I are in the waiting room at Ultra-clinical's office the next day. She's a neurologist. She'll examine me and order the hospital stay and IV, per Nice-doctor. We wait, wait, wait for hours while my head shakes like one of those bobbing heads in the rear window of a car.

The clinicals are in charge; I must be patient. My life revolves around them now. They say, "Jump" and I ask, "How high?" I know they're trying to help me.

Finally, we're called in. I look around the examination room. She's taped her children's drawings to the wall. I wistfully recall the simplicity of childhood.

Ultra-clinical enters the room. She's a former researcher who didn't major in bedside manners. She pokes and prods scientifically.

"Let's see," she says. "Maybe it isn't MS."

MS loves it. *Tricking doctors is fun! That's right. Don't treat her right off. Hey, guys, I'll make sure that not all the symptoms point to us, at first. That'll make the diagnosis difficult.*

*Great idea*, the Little Helpers chortle. *That'll give us more time to lunch on Sue's brain, unhindered. Let's have a picnic, everyone!*

"Bear with me while I run some tests," Ultra-clinical says.

She hooks me up to some electrodes and sends electricity through my muscles. They jump and scream in protest, reminding me of medieval torture. Jeff leaves the exam room. He can't bear to watch.

Sure, we'll bear with you, Ultra-clinical. What else can we do?

The Little Helpers have a party in my brain for the next four months, while tests are conducted.

*This is a ball*, they say. *Tenderloin is delectable for dinner. We've been in this spot before. Chomp, chomp. Uh-oh, we chewed too hard. These nerve cells are severed.*

MS smiles. *That'll make the tremors permanent. But don't tell anyone, Little Helpers. We'll keep this under our hats for a while.*

## THE KILLER CANE

My head keeps bobbing along, but not like that robin everyone sings about. The tremors cause goose egg-sized knots in my shoulder and back muscles. I fetch the apparatus for my new nightly ritual.

A fetching medium-blue, it looks like a cane, with a hard plastic knob on the end of the curved part. The straight part has a handle on it. I flip the curved part over my shoulder, pull on the handle and feel the plastic knob dig into the muscles in my back and shoulders. The pressure forces the knots to release. My muscles feel black-and-blue.

A modern form of torture that brings tears to my eyes, I nickname this delightful device the "Killer Cane." What a way to spend every evening!

## BACK TO THE FAMILIAR?

This is too unfamiliar. I know! I can go back to work. Would that be OK, Ultra-clinical? "Sure," she says. "It might be good for you."

A month after the tremors started, I sit at my desk trying to read some data from a report. I need to transfer it to my computer's spreadsheet program. I'm frustrated. My eyes struggle to refocus with every jerk of my head. My muscles scream. I want to scream, too. Why is this happening to me?

One of my coworkers pokes her head into my office. "Can I help you?" she asks sympathetically.

"Yeah, I sure could use some help," I gratefully reply. "My job isn't so easy to do anymore. Thanks for the assist."

After she leaves, my heart sinks. My days at the VA are numbered.

Uh-oh, the director is looking at me. I know what he's thinking by the expression on his face: *She's a goner, no longer fit for executive management. That's too bad. She looked really promising.*

MS snickers. *Her life is falling apart. Just what I wanted! Before long I'll have all of her and she'll be totally helpless.*

The Little Helpers are fixated on their feast. *If we chew right here, she won't be able to swallow anymore. Wait, we'll save that for dessert. Let's keep to the main menu for now.*

"It's not so bad," Ultra-clinical says. "Just a few tremors. It could be worse."

I invite her to live in my body for a while. She declines.

## PUNISHED FOR BEING SICK

I weep as I work on some disability retirement paperwork. What? I receive only 33 percent of my pay? I thought I'd receive 70 percent. That's why Jeff and I didn't get catastrophic insurance. This is a catastrophe!

I feel like I'm being punished for being sick. But what can I do? The rules are the rules.

My huge cache of sick time, then vacation time, dwindles to nothing. Many of my colleagues donate vacation time. One of the doctors gives a week's worth. Amazed and humbled, I profusely thank them all. Their kindness allows me to remain at full pay until October 1996. The VA's been good to me these past seventeen years.

## WHO IS THAT?

I stand at the bedroom mirror and look at myself. Who is that? She doesn't look familiar at all. She's shaking from head to toe and wearing a cervical collar. The intense tremors sometimes make her head whip violently. The cervical collar keeps her from giving herself whiplash.

# Chapter Three

## THE MS ROLLER COASTER

CHOMP, CHOMP. THE Little Helpers are munching again. *OK, Sue's head tremor means we've done some damage. Now if we try this tasty spot over here, her right shoulder will start jerking.*

MS nods in approval. *Yeah. That's what I like to see.*

Ultra-clinical comes back from a California conference. I see some emotion; her eyes fill with tears.

"I'm so sorry! I'm so sorry!" she says. It's good to see her heart.

She reverts to clinical mode. "The shoulder jerking is called rubral tremor. It indicates that your condition is worsening more rapidly than I had anticipated," she says. "It's time for something radical. I'm ordering a methylprednisolone IV. You'll receive it for five days, as an outpatient at the hospital. We'll talk again afterwards."

MS says, *No, no. Leave us to our work. Do not disturb.*

The Little Helpers make a grimace. *That steroid IV tastes awful. Five days is too much, we're getting sleepy. Time for a little siesta.*

I still have tremors after the five days of treatment. Maybe it isn't going to work.

Is there such a thing as hell on earth? I think I've discovered it. Jeff joins me there. Oh, no! He shouldn't have to suffer, too.

### THE TREMORS STOP!

Yes! We have success! A few days after the IV, the tremors stop. It feels weird not to shake. Jeff stands still while I grab his hands and dance around the living room. I'm free! I'm free!

Relief. Joy. Rest. These are good things, and they are mine.

I make plans. I can stop the retirement process and go back to work. My life is back on track.

I call Mom. Why don't we have a party this weekend? We can celebrate my brother's birthday and my newfound freedom.

MS rubs its eyes. The effects of the IV treatment are wearing off. *That was a good snooze, but now it's time to get back to work. Be quiet about it, though, little guys. We don't want anyone to know we're awake again. Stealth is a hallmark of mine. Let's keep it between you and me for now.*

The Little Helpers respond immediately. *Ooh-la-la! This part of Sue's brain has a particularly piquant quality, almost spicy. It's exciting!*

I return to Ultra-clinical for a follow-up visit. Jeff and I are happy. She pokes and prods.

As she stares at me, I suddenly become aware that my head is moving up and down ever so slightly. I concentrate on holding my head still so she can agree with us that the tremor is gone.

Frowning, she says, "I can still detect a slight tremor."

"But the IV has helped you," she continues. "That means you have MS."

Our happiness balloon deflates with a loud, *Pfffffpt!*

MS says, *Welcome to my roller coaster, Sue and Jeff. One moment you're very up, and the next moment you're very down.*

Launching into clinical terminology, Ultra-clinical explains. "The IV methylprednisolone was given to suppress your body's immune system. Your brain, spinal cord and optic nerves have a separate, very weak immune system because of the delicate nature of the tissue in those areas.

"The blood-brain barrier separates the two immune systems. MS has compromised your blood-brain barrier. You might say there's a hole in it. As a result, your body's immune system components are now in those areas of delicate tissue. Having never encountered this tissue before, they identify it as foreign matter that must be destroyed.

"For reasons we don't yet understand, they concentrate their attack on the myelin sheaths that cover the nerve cells. As a result, your brain, spinal cord, and optic nerves short-circuit, resulting in the multiple types of symptoms that you're experiencing.

"MS is incurable, but if we can suppress your immune system, we can slow the progression of the disease. It seems like the steroid IV is doing its job. Let's taper off with an oral steroid called prednisone."

## FUTURE? WHAT FUTURE?

Most of Ultra-clinical's words are Greek to me. "You have MS" is very understandable, though. My neighbor comes to mind again, and Aunt Dot. Future? What future? I don't even want to think about it.

What will Jeff do? His right leg was amputated after he was shot in Vietnam during the war. I can't help him anymore. How will he ever help me?

Ultra-clinical also prescribes Avonex to suppress my body's immune system. Jeff and I must administer the injections ourselves. We look at each other incredulously.

Arranging for injection training and the first shipment of Avonex will take some time. Then, once a week, I'll thrust a long intramuscular needle into my thigh and push the plunger. Flu-like symptoms will sicken me within a few hours. Then, for the next twenty-four hours, severe headache, body aches, and fever will buffet my body. The intensity of my tremors and other MS symptoms will temporarily increase, too.

Jeff is overjoyed that the steroid IV worked. He exclaims, "Having you better is like winning the lottery!"

I can live with the Avonex side effects. It feels good to see Jeff happy for a change.

## MS ROLLS IN THE AISLES

A few nights later, I wake up in Tremor City. I thought I'd left that town for good.

Do I hear laughing in there?

MS is rolling in the aisles. *Ha-ha. Me and My Little Helpers woke up from our quick nap a while ago, and you didn't know it. I see the tremors woke Jeff. That's great! Weep for hours together. Now you two can be terrorized in tandem.*

I call Mom to give her the bad news—the tremors are back. I know, it shouldn't happen to me. I don't deserve it. But here they are, anyway. We cry together.

Family gatherings should be happy, but this one isn't. Sue's new lease on life just ran out. Hey, landlord, it's not fair.

Ultra-clinical says she can temporarily increase the prednisone dose, but only for a little while. Launching into clinical mode, she says, "If I prescribe it for you long-term, it will cause osteoporosis and high blood pressure. It will also thin the mucous membranes in your esophagus, lungs, and other mucous-lined areas. Oh, yes, it also raises your blood sugar and can cause glaucoma and mania. Finally," she says, "there's the possibility of Cushing's syndrome."

Floored, I stare at her. I'm willing do anything to shut down the tremors, though.

MS dozes because of the high dose of prednisone prescribed by Ultra-clinical.

"Let's try some other things," Ultra-clinical says.

She tapers me off the prednisone. The tremors bounce back with a vengeance.

Zoned out on Valium, then Klonopin and a plethora of other medications, I've become a walking drugstore. Nothing works. Shake, shake, shake go my head and right shoulder. My back joins in now. I bounce at the waist when I bend over.

## My, My! It's Myoclonus

MS is in stitches. *This is so much fun! Feast away, my friends.*

The Little Helpers say, *That spinal cord was especially tasty. Let's go back there for a while. Oops, now her legs are trembling wildly.*

The floor feels like it's moving up and down when I stand, as if I'm walking through a fun house. But this is definitely not fun.

I tell Ultra-clinical about the bouncing floor beneath me.

She says, "Lie on the table and give me your left foot."

She helps me onto the table. I maneuver my left leg into position. She takes my foot in her hand.

"Now push as hard as you can," she commands.

Hey, what's happening? My leg is pumping rapidly. I didn't tell it to do that. It has a mind of its own.

"That's called myoclonus," Ultra-clinical says.

My, oh my. It's myoclonus, another MS symptom. This one indicates that paralysis is well on its way.

Suddenly, my left leg is paralyzed. Pressing into the flesh is like pressing on a piece of meat at the supermarket. It doesn't belong to me anymore.

Hey, things are moving too fast. Many years should pass before MS accelerates. I'm supposed to have a break in the action from time to time. My remission is missin'. Let's form a search party.

MS says, *It's time for some Tex-Mex, Little Helpers. That'll put a stop to her line dancing forever.*

They lick their chops with delight and dig in.

Suddenly, I have brick feet. They aren't mine anymore. I can't feel a thing in them or under them.

MS gives me a good hard poke in my bladder. *That'll be embarrassing*, it sneers. My dignity crumples.

The Little Helpers join in. *If we chew right here, her bladder will act really crazy and spasm painfully*, they say.

MS smiles. *Thanks, guys. Pain's the name of our game.*

# Chapter Four

# THE HEARTACHE HOTEL

I KNOW WHERE YOU live, MS. The diagnosis is now official, no longer tentative. We know you're in there. Ultra-clinical made the call. We see your fingerprints everywhere. Now I can come out of my corner fighting.

MS isn't scared. *No one knows what to do to stop me. I'm incurable.*

The Little Helpers whisper, *The man downstairs will help us keep her in her place, too. Time to graze at this cute little snack bar over here. Life is good!*

## DIVORCE?

Living with a wife with MS is too much to ask of Jeff. I offer him a divorce.

I take his hands in my hands and say, "I don't want you to have MS with me, Jeff. You don't deserve this."

Jeff pauses and says, "You're not going to get rid of me that easily."

The offer was serious, but we decide our marriage is too love-filled to let MS end it.

Jeff says, "Let's do something normal."

We haven't used that adjective for a long time.

MS rubs its hands. *This will be fun. Neither one of them knows that "normal" has been out of the picture entirely since the moment her tremors began. Yuk, yuk.*

We grab a pizza and a video, *The Bridges of Madison County.* We don't yet realize we've chosen a weepy movie. Oh, no, here come the waterworks. Melancholy washes over us like a wave. We're drowning in it. No matter how hard we try, we can't escape the overarching specter of MS.

Clapping its hands with glee, MS declares, *I'm your new reality. I won't settle for less than all of your attention, all the time.*

The pizza sets like a rock in our stomachs. So much for doing something normal.

## AND MY RESEARCH REVEALS...

MS has a board meeting with the Little Helpers. They're attentive but insatiably hungry. *Sue's doing research on the Internet*, MS says. *She's going to find out about us. Let's be quiet and watch as she reads the bad news.*

The Little Helpers cry, *Oh, look at the expression on her face!*

MS deftly delivers an uppercut. Down for the count, I stare at the web page. There's more pain to come, and more symptoms are on their way. Here's a total paralysis chaser, just for a little extra challenge. You won't die of MS, but you'll choke to death.

I swallow hard. I might not be able to do that later.

## MY POCKETBOOK TAKES ANOTHER HIT

MS has already robbed me of my comfortable paycheck; in November 1996, it hits me in the pocketbook again. My legs are worse. Climbing the three stairs that lead to the front door has become a serious challenge. I'm using forearm crutches to help me walk and keep my balance.

We spend our nest egg and my inheritance from Dad to add a garage and connecting foyer onto our home. The construction crew works diligently, sliding nervous sideways glances at me as I thrash around on the La-Z-Boy. The work is done by Christmas.

The garage has an attractive wheelchair ramp inside, and the wide garage door is tall enough to accommodate a wheelchair-accessible van. Things are going to get worse, we know.

## MY HEAD HURTS

Meanwhile, the Little Helpers are not-so-quietly nibbling away on my brain. *Mmm, good!* they cry.

Groan! My head hurts all the time. Pills don't help. Headache becomes my new constant companion. I press both hands down onto the top of my head. When I let up, the pain comes back. I lie on the La-Z-Boy, in agony.

Ultra-clinical says, "Headache usually indicates onset of an MS exacerbation. I'll watch you closely. Let's do another round of IVs, too."

## ISN'T THAT PATHETIC?

Jeff is the chef and housekeeper now. I can't help. A house cleaner comes every two weeks to help him with the cleaning, and teenagers help outdoors. We pay them out of our meager income.

Sitting on the deck in my special high-backed lawn chair, I wistfully watch the teens. Strangers work in my beloved gardens.

Going to the grocery store is an adventure these days. When I wake up in the morning, I feel like I've already run a marathon. Add that fatigue to my leg symptoms, and voilá! My new shopping assistant is an electric cart.

I finally figure out how to drive it so I can stop terrorizing the other customers. A little old lady skitters to the side; she remembers the day I almost ran her down. Stock boys run to the aisles, recalling how many times I've knocked over displays.

I stop my cart and rest on an especially shaky day. A woman at the other end of the aisle looks at me.

"Isn't that pathetic?" she asks no one in particular.

Silently offended, I wonder why she called me a "that."

## TOO MUCH TO HANDLE

My new home is the Heartache Hotel. "MS is too much for me to handle," I tell Jeff. "I need to go to the support group at the hospital. An online friend told me about it. You're wonderful, but I need to talk with people who are going through what I'm going through. Will you come with me to the meetings?"

He agrees. I call the group facilitator. She records my demographics in typical clinical style. She's very friendly, though. "See you on Thursday."

I meet Debbie Hutchinson. Hey, she was in my brother's high school class. Her husband, John, smiles broadly. They aren't fooling us, though. We can see their melancholy shroud, sewn by the fingers of MS. We compare the workmanship in theirs versus ours; each has a slightly different weave, but they are equally grotesque.

## MS SISTERS

Debbie is my new friend now, thanks to the support group. Our daily telephone conversations are a relief to me. She's like a sister. We share MS.

MS chuckles. *Share all you want. My Little Helpers are still munching on both of you. I'm incurable; you can't get rid of me. Go ahead, make me the center of your lives.*

Debbie says, "Would you like to come to church with us?"

Hmm. Jeff didn't like it the last time I talked about church. I don't think so, Debbie. Thanks for offering, though.

The man downstairs says, *Yes! That's what I like to hear. I'm preparing a place for you, Sue, and it's the hottest nightspot around. See you soon!*

# Chapter Five

## DRAWING NEAR

MORE GENTLE INVITATIONS come from Debbie. "Our church is holding a spaghetti supper. Do you want to come with John and me?" she asks.

Jeff is a spaghetti fan. We decide to go.

Hey, these people are friendly. They don't mind my tremors and the other MS symptoms.

I wanted to come back to church a couple of years ago. I think this is the one.

I announce to Jeff, "I want to attend Debbie's church. You can drop me off at the service or come in."

MS is aghast. *Keep her away from there! My Little Helpers made it so she can't drive anymore. Don't drive her, Jeff. She'll hear some Good News there, and it might just ruin our fun.*

The Little Helpers chime in. *This Jesus stuff might interrupt our meal. That's not polite.*

Jeff calculates that he would only have fifteen minutes at home between dropping me off and picking me up. "I might as well stay for the service," he says.

### CLANK! THAT'S MY HARD HEART

The first Sunday evening at Debbie's church, Pastor Alan Witter is preaching. His words sound absurd to me. They conflict with my treasured opinions. In a voice so loud that everyone in the church can hear it, I turn to Jeff and scoff at what the pastor is teaching.

We return the following week anyway. Debbie and John are our friends. Pastor Alan and Barbara are likable and the congregation warmly welcomed us. Ah, this week's sermon is more my cup of tea.

Clank! A word from Pastor Alan bounces off my hard heart.

A few weeks later, I visit the parsonage. While Barbara buzzes around the kitchen, she tells me she talks with Jesus. How weird is that? And she says Jesus answers her. Weirder still!

MS shouts, *Don't listen to them! Go back home. Don't get near them. They can't help you. No one can help you. You're too fatigued to go to church.*

The Little Helpers pause between bites to join in the shouting, but I refuse to listen to them. I want to hear what Pastor Alan and Barbara are saying.

## A Word Gets into My Heart

Clank, clank. Tunk. Tunk? Hey, what's that? Oh! A word from Pastor Alan penetrates my heart. I catch a fleeting glimpse of Jesus Christ. He doesn't look like all the other gods. He's the Son of the one true God, and He loves me.

Jesus says, "Come to Me, all who are weary and heavy-laden, and I will give you rest. Take My yoke upon you and learn from Me, for I am gentle and humble in heart, and you will find rest for your souls. For My yoke is easy and my burden is light" (see Matthew 11:28–30).

Jesus, I am weary and have a burden. Will You give me rest?

We sing a hymn and Jeff and I weep. Someone is touching our hearts.

MS is furious and delivers a one-two punch to my face.

I'm hurt but still standing. The one-two punch supplies me with more pain, worse headaches, more muscle spasticity and paralysis, and tremors, tremors, tremors.

The Little Helpers are busy. They gorge themselves in an all-out eating contest.

Sorry, guys. You aren't keeping me away from church.

Debbie blesses me by fashioning a flexible backboard so I can bear to sit in the pew. I rest my head against its soft blue padding.

The backboard's springiness softens the effects of my head's violent jerking.

A few weeks later, Pastor Alan comes to our house for coffee. We are on our best behavior.

He asks, "Have you ever thought about joining the church?"

We like the idea. Thanks, Pastor Alan. We want to join.

We take the classes and learn what grace is. Rebels without a cause now believe Jesus died for their sins and rose again. We aren't sure what that last part means to us yet. The congregation welcomes us as new members.

We confess Jesus as our Savior, and the Father forgives us. We don't yet know it, but the Holy Spirit begins His work in our hearts.

We begin to believe the Bible is true. We feel God's presence when we sing. Though my body informs me that MS still attacking and munching, I'm turning my attention to Jesus.

MS and the Little Helpers cry, *Oh, no! This Good News sure isn't good news for us.*

# Chapter Six

## NEXT STOP BOSTON

MS PREPARES TO launch an assault against my newfound faith. *She just* thinks *she's able to cope with my attacks. It's time to reveal my long-kept secret about the tremors.*

The Little Helpers chortle, *Meanwhile, we'll find a new spot for dinner. Maybe a little teriyaki would be good. We love take-out.*

Ultra-clinical sends Jeff and me to Brigham and Women's MS Clinic in Boston. It's not a good sign. She's run out of ideas.

"Maybe you'll qualify for a research trial there," she says hopefully.

The MS Clinic staff is testing new treatments for MS. Maybe they'll be able to help me. Jeff and I aren't too confident, though. We've seen too many hopes dashed.

The waiting room at the MS Clinic is crowded with my fellow sufferers. Wheelchairs, walkers, and crutches accompany them. I look around at blank faces, eyes filled with hopelessness. Join the crowd, Sue.

Research-clinical is our next stop. He has kind eyes, but he's all business.

We're taping our meeting. Ultra-clinical wants details, and we anticipated we wouldn't be able to write fast enough to catch all that Research-clinical will tell us.

After he examines me, he says, "I'm sorry to say you're not going to have any more relief from MS. You have a progressive form of the disease."

What? Wait a minute! You just shot down my paper airplane. It had the word *hope* scrawled on it, in very small letters. Mayday! Mayday! I watch as it crashes to the carpet with a soft "whoosh."

Research-clinical continues, "You began with a relapsing/remitting form of the disease, back in your twenties. Now it is secondary/progressive. I like to call it "relapsing/progressive." We're still working on the names of the different stages of MS. We don't fully understand the disease."

There's more bad news from Research-clinical. "You don't qualify for the Betaseron/Copaxone trial. That's only for relapsing/remitting forms of MS."

Gulp. I wait for the rest of the story.

Research-clinical continues, "We can't do anything for your tremors. You've had axonal burnout. That means nerve cell axons in your brain have been severed. The tremors are permanent."

MS delivers two roundhouse punches, one to Jeff and one to me. Our heads spin. I fall down to the mat, then crawl to my corner. Jeff is still bravely standing, but his lip is trembling and I see a tear in his eye.

I hear the Little Helpers again. They're partying heartily. *The secret's out! We did the damage a long time ago, but she's just now learning it's permanent! Hee hee.*

## A SLIGHT HOPE

Research-clinical has an idea. "I'm doing a trial right now of Cytoxan/methylprednisolone pulse therapy. It's chemotherapy, administered once a month for the first year, then once every six weeks in the second year, once every two months in the third year, and so on, for a total of five years. It can cause bladder cancer, though we haven't had that happen in our research trial so far."

MS screeches, *No! Chemotherapy might shut down our operation for a while. Be afraid of bladder cancer, Sue. You don't want cancer. You have enough to do, dealing with us.*

Jeff and I lapse into information overload. There are too many words to process: *progressive, irreversible, axonal burnout, chemotherapy.*

MS begins its victory dance.

Jeff wonders how long it will be before he can't take care of me anymore, and asks, "Should we plan for Sue to be in a nursing home within five years?"

"That would be a reasonable expectation," Research-clinical says. "The prognosis is not good. Tremor usually indicates a rapid downhill course of the disease."

## Lost in Boston

After we leave his office, we try to drive out of Boston. We're lost for four hours. Fading fast, I say, "I need to take a pill, Jeff, but I don't have any water. Please stop at that VA over there."

Jeff seeks water in the blood-spattered ER. I wander in. My tremors have gone wild. I don't see any available chairs. I slide down onto the floor and lean my back and head against a glass wall. My head bump, bump, bumps against it. Jeff brings me a cup of water.

The staff helps Jeff phone his brother, Kevin, in Lexington. Kevin sends out rescuers June and Ben to retrieve us. We leave Boston, wishing we were leaving forever.

After an overnight stay at Kevin's place, we return home. It's a quiet ride. We're both in shock and still reeling at the prospect of our dismal future. Research-clinical's words replay endlessly in our minds.

At home, we discuss our options. We decide I have nothing to lose by participating in the research trial.

## Rugged Terrain

I begin chemotherapy. The terrain is rugged, the side effects painful and exhausting. Intense nausea comes with every treatment. My MS symptoms temporarily magnify, and severe fatigue washes over me.

MS goes to sleep, but not the tremors. They're permanent and relentless.

The Little Helpers say, *Yech! That Cytoxan tastes worse than the steroid IV. The bad taste will fade, though. We're feeling very sleepy. Hey, we can still enjoy a midnight snack between snoozes.*

*We'll just nibble slowly and be really quiet as we polish off this portion. That way no one will know we're still doing damage.*

My white blood cells crash to dangerous levels after every chemotherapy treatment. Until my count comes back up, my ability to fight bacteria and viruses is nil. I don a mask when my count is high enough for me to safely attend church. Jeff is my protector, fending off everyone who wants to hug me.

Attention, Sue, you are now entering Isolation City, a very lonely place. I consider isolation a small price to pay for feeling better, though. Most of my MS symptoms have receded.

# Chapter Seven

## STEPPING OFF A CLIFF

I CHANGE TO A new neurologist, Nice-clinical. He treats Jeff and me like royalty and his staff handles all the details. No more legwork for Sue--a good thing because her legs still don't work very well, and she's very easily fatigued.

Can we do my chemotherapy in Maine, Nice-clinical? The Boston trips are very taxing.

He says, "I don't see why not. I'll make the arrangements."

No more Boston trips, thank God. Jeff is relieved. Boston's traffic was terrific.

### LOSING MY MIND

I can't think of words anymore, even simple ones. I don't remember how to reconcile my checking account. My foggy memory vaguely visualizes Sue the computer specialist, corporate trainer, statistician, wearer of many hats. That girl is gone. Her image fades into the mist.

Word Search puzzles strain my brain. I use a ruler to track the letters because my jerking head makes it nearly impossible for me to focus my eyes on the pages. Reading a book is out of the question.

The Little Helpers gleefully continue their feast. *Midnight snacks are indeed fun, fellas! This visual processing area looks delish! If we chew there, images on the TV screen will move around too much for her. She'll get dizzy and nauseated and won't be able to watch it anymore.*

MS rejoices. *Perfect! It's time for her to turn her full attention to us.*

## Stepping Off a Cliff

It's 1999, and I'm in my second year of chemotherapy. Out of the blue, intense bouts of vomiting follow every treatment. Cytoxan's toxicity has built up in my body. Vomit City is a very unpleasant place to visit.

We make the now-familiar trek to the ER. The clinicals look at me with sympathy, and administer IV fluids to relieve my severe dehydration.

The positive effects from the chemotherapy no longer outweigh the side effects.

"Jeff, can I quit?" I ask plaintively. "I don't have cancer, after all. Maybe the chemotherapy has permanently slowed the MS."

"It's up to you, hon. I hate to watch you suffer," he says.

MS rejoices. *She's stopping the chemotherapy. We'll have free rein in her brain again!*

The Little Helpers add, *We can invite all our friends for a block party. Who wants to send out the invitations?*

When I stop the chemotherapy, I step off a cliff. I didn't see it coming. Now I'm in free fall with no helpful branch to grab onto. I pick up speed. All my symptoms rocket to new heights while I plummet into who-knows-what's-next.

I scare my friends at the MS support group. Nice-clinical describes my tremors as "gross." They certainly are. A recliner is needed for Sue; she can't sit up in a regular chair for the meetings anymore.

I thrash around in the recliner while my MS friends look on in horror.

## No Hope

Nice-clinical prescribes a new a pill, Neurontin, when I first start seeing him. The drug tames the tremors through the day, when I first start taking it. If I really concentrate, I can hold my head still. The tremors overwhelm me by evening, though.

MS says, *Not so fast. I want to harass her all day and all night. Go get her, Little Helpers.*

They gorge themselves some more. It only takes a couple of weeks for the tremors to break through the Neurontin during the day.

"Let's try increasing the dose," Nice-clinical says.

The tremors crash the gates again. How about a higher dose? They still break through.

MS is guffawing. *She'll come to the end of her rope soon. Then she'll just give up and let me have my way with her.*

Wait just a minute, MS. I have a secret weapon. I'm asking Jesus to help me cope. He said He'd carry my MS burden.

*Oh, no, not Jesus!* MS cries. *Get away from Him. You're beyond help now.*

Sorry, I'm looking at Jesus. Distractions are arranged.

The Little Helpers say, *Look here. We've found a new noshing nook. We can't think of a better taste bud-tickler.*

Now I can't think at all. My mind turns to mush. Nice-clinical sends me to Neuropsych-guy for evaluation. His assistant puts me through my paces with several lengthy sessions of frustrating tests.

Reviewing the findings, Neuropsych-guy says, "You have cognitive dysfunction and have lost executive function. That's the ability to do more than one task at a time."

The results confirm what I already know. She who elevated multitasking to an art form is long gone.

I pay another visit to Nice-clinical on December 11, 2000. I have no good news for him, and he has no good news for me. My eyes well up with tears as friends drive me back home. There's no hope. Stop the presses. No more writing in my MS journal.

Jesus, help me deal with all of this!

# Chapter Eight

## ENTER JESUS

### A Testimony of Healing

PASTOR ALAN IS in the pulpit. He and Barbara are on their way to Nigeria as missionaries. They want to give us their testimony before they go.

While in Haiti as missionaries, Alan had a sudden, severe pain in his head. Barbara noted Alan's symptoms; they matched that of a burst brain aneurysm.

Barbara and another missionary couple laid hands on Alan and prayed. "Jesus, heal Alan. Seal up the aneurysm. In Your name we pray."

Alan recovered. As quickly as arrangements could be made, they flew to a hospital in Pennsylvania. A brain scan showed an aneurysm had burst and then sealed itself. Barbara and Alan praised God.

How about that? I'm glad He helped them but I don't believe divine healing is an option for me. I'm incurable.

MS jumps up and down for joy. *She knows she's beyond help*, it cries.

### A Song in the Night

A few days pass. In the middle of the night, I suddenly wake up. A melody and lyrics to a song are playing in my mind. Where did that come from?

Jesus, is that You? You're saying what? I had troubles and strife, but now You've come. When You showed me Your grace and love, my soul healed. My life is complete now. I'm whole. I'll serve you,

33

Lord, body and soul. I've found the joy of Your love and I must share it. Help me spread the Good News everywhere.

I struggle out of bed and find the tape recorder so I can record the song. I might not remember it tomorrow.

I call Barbara and exclaim, "Jesus gave me a song!"

"Praise the Lord," she cries.

After I sing it to her, she asks, "Would you sing it on Sunday at our music ministry time?"

"Sure," I say, "but you know I can't stand up and I haven't played my guitar for years."

"That's all right, we'll get a chair for you," she says. "Jesus will help you sing and play."

On Sunday, I sit in a chair at the front of the church, plunking on my guitar and singing weakly. Use me, O Lord. I'm in your hands, that I may help others to understand. Use me, Lord, show me what to do, that Lord, I may draw others closer to You.

MS shudders. The news is not good for it and its Little Helpers. They enter Panic City.

I think I just heard a, "Hallelujah!" from heaven.

## PASTOR DOC ARRIVES

The new pastor, David "Doc" Uber, arrives in January 2001. He was given the nickname "Doc" because he used to drink like Doc Holliday. He kept the nickname, but now it means "Disciple of Christ." Jesus transformed him, healed him of his addiction, and set him free.

I hear MS screaming, *Don't listen to him!*

Too late, MS. Jeff and I hear him preach and he bowls us over. He speaks with power. What's this he's saying about God being bigger than we think?

# "READ THIS BOOK! IT WILL CHANGE YOUR LIFE!"

We fly to Florida to seek some respite from winter. The weather is warm and sunny, but it doesn't help me feel better. We stay with relatives since we can't afford hotels.

The Florida branch of the family thinks I'm going to die while I'm visiting them. They're just not used to my symptoms. My jerking head, seismic tremors and staggering make them uneasy and fearful as they helplessly watch. We return to Maine after a few weeks.

In March, I'm at a meeting in New York. Superintendent Wil Sharpe's wife, Debbie, speaks to the group.

She holds up a little book called *The Prayer of Jabez*, by Bruce Wilkinson, and fervently urges us all, "Read this book. It will change your life!"

I buy it when I get home. I read that Jabez was more honorable than his brothers. He asked God to bless him and God did (see 1 Chronicles 4:9). I always thought asking God to bless me was selfish.

What harm can it do, though? Jabez prayed and God blessed. I pray the prayer every day. Lord, bless me indeed, enlarge my territory, keep Your hand upon me and keep me from harm (see 1 Chronicles 4:10).

MS and the Little Helpers stagger into their corner and collapse on the stool.

The man downstairs bellows, *Don't give up! I don't want her to be the one that got away. I'll get some help.*

## CHASING GOD

A few weeks later, our church board meets. Jeff and I are members and are in our usual places. Pastor Doc hands each board member *The God Chasers*, by Tommy Tenney.

He says, "I could have written this book. Every one of us should have an intimate relationship with the Lord."

The board members look at each other, puzzled. They flip through the book's pages.

After the meeting, I decide to read the book. Its message grips me. Can I know God that way?

I know, I'll pray and see. Slide off the couch onto the floor, Sue. Roll over onto your stomach. It's hard, but you can do it. Pray every day, "I want to know You like that, Lord!" Weep. Crawl back over to the couch. Grab on and pull yourself up. Whew! I'm exhausted.

The book makes me hungry, but not for regular food. A change of diet is in order. I want the Bread of Life, Christ Himself. Nothing else will satisfy me now. I want all of You, God!

The man downstairs calls for the medics.

In its corner, MS has fainted dead away. There are little "x's" over its eyes. The Little Helpers bawl for their battered boss.

## A STARTLING WORD

Pastor Doc speaks from the pulpit on a Sunday in April 2001.

"I'm sticking my neck out. I've had a vision, and in it, Debbie and Sue are healed."

Wait, that's not for today. Hey, I feel my face lighting up. What's going on? I smile broadly. Could it be?

Debbie and I continue on, as if Pastor Doc never spoke. We're sisters in MS, walking arm-in-arm through our nightmare.

## HEY, DEATH, YOU DIDN'T GET ME

On July 3, 2001, I nearly die. An ambulance is called when I collapse in the Sears department store. By the time I arrive at the ER I'm in rigor, right next door to rigor mortis.

The man downstairs is having trouble reviving MS; it's out cold from all that Jesus stuff. The Little Helpers need some assistance. He sends a blood infection into the boxing ring to keep me down until MS is on its feet again. The clinicals can't find the infection's source.

Pastor Doc sits by my hospital bed every day, praying. His presence comforts me.

The IV antibiotic isn't working. I'm still very feverish and close to death. Visitors come, pay their respects, and leave with tear-filled eyes.

Family-doctor comes in visibly alarmed, and orders a second IV antibiotic. The fever breaks. Hey, Death, you didn't get me.

MS roars back to life, thanks to my weakened condition from the infection. Lunging from its corner, it flails its fists at me. I can't count the punches.

Satan dances for joy. *Thanks, MS. It's good to have you back on the team. She's no longer hell-bound, but I can still make her life hellish.*

## DOES GOD STILL HEAL?

Just before I'm discharged from the hospital, Pastor Doc asks, "Do you think God still heals?"

I reply confidently, "No, healing isn't for today. Jesus only healed people back in biblical times. Today's 'healers' are just charlatans."

Frowning, he says, "OK." Then he nods kindly. "I'll see you later, Sue."

On his knees at home, he prays, "Lord, are you sure this is the one?"

Jesus says to him, "It's time to phone Sue."

Pastor Doc obeys. "May I come over with my guitar?" he asks me. "We can play music and sing, look at some scriptures on healing, and pray."

I ask Jeff. "I guess there's no harm in it," he says.

I answer Pastor Doc. "Yes, you can come."

Jeff ponders his offer. What does this guy want from us? Money?

# Chapter Nine

# HEART PREPARATION

Pastor Doc tells me two things are required for entry onto the highway to healing. He won't begin working with me until they're done.

He begins. "Here's the first thing. Are you right with God? Do you willfully disobey Him?"

Hey, what kind of question is that? I go to church. I believe in Jesus. Though briefly offended, I know I need to pray.

At night, I lie on my bed, alone. I feel timid as I ask, "Lord, am I right with you?"

I don't hear an answer.

The next day, I report what happened to Pastor Doc. Since I didn't hear an answer from the Lord, I guess I must be right with Him.

## FORGIVING THE UNFORGIVABLE

Pastor Doc says, "OK. Here's the second thing. Do you have unforgiveness in your heart? Are you holding any grudges?"

Oh, yeah. First Husband immediately comes to mind. He beat me up and ran off with another woman.

Pastor Doc says, "You know what to do."

I pray that night and God gives me the ability to forgive First Husband. I know it in my heart. The bitterness is gone. I report to Pastor Doc.

"Good!" he says. "Now we're ready to begin. Let's set a date. How's July 26 at 2 p.m.?"

My calendar is clear for that day. I make a note: "2 p.m. Pastor Doc and Sue guitars."

## THE FIRST VISIT

Pastor Doc rings the doorbell. I hobble to the door and swing it open. Sunlight streams in behind him. He's loaded down with a guitar, a Bible and some three-ring binders.

Come in. Coffee? Let's sit here at the dining room table.

Jeff is in the den. He's keeping his distance, a victim of too many hopes shot down. He doesn't believe Jesus heals, but maybe Pastor Doc's visits will help me somehow.

Pastor Doc looks at me across the table. His blue eyes pierce me through.

He says, "Let's sing. Do you know any contemporary Christian music?"

"Not really," I reply nervously. "I know a few hymns, and a couple of contemporary songs Pastor Alan and Barbara taught the children at our church."

"These are easy," he says, and begins playing and singing.

I catch on quickly. My spirit lifts as I praise God. I like the feeling.

MS doesn't. It screams, *Oh, no! She's worshiping!*

The Little Helpers cry, *We're being poisoned! Call an ambulance!*

The man downstairs is nowhere to be seen. He can't stand the love.

"Let's look at the Bible," Pastor Doc says. "Go to Hebrews 13:8."

I have no idea that the Book of Hebrews exists, let alone where it's located.

"Can you show me where that is, Pastor Doc?" I ask.

It only takes him a few seconds to flip my Bible to the passage. He commands, "Read it."

I read it to myself. Jesus Christ is the same yesterday, today and forever. I look up at Pastor Doc.

"No," he says. "Read it out loud. Faith comes by hearing and hearing by the Word of God."

I read it out loud. Now I'm embarrassed. Jesus didn't stop

working after He hung on a cross two thousand years ago and rose again. He's alive and still doing what He did then. I thought He wasn't healing anymore.

Pastor Doc says, "Do you see any time limits?"

I blush and meekly say no.

MS is in Desperation City now. *She's listening intently. She's not questioning what he says. She's hearing the truth!*

The Little Helpers are frenzied. *What will we do now?* they cry.

## WHO HAS BELIEVED OUR MESSAGE?

Pastor Doc takes me to Isaiah 53:1. I read, "Who has believed our message? And to whom has the arm of the Lord been revealed?"

He explains, "The arm of the Lord, His power, is revealed to the ones who believe the message." He pauses, then asks, "Do you believe the message?"

Intrigued, I say, "Tell me more."

He continues. "Look at verse 4. Jesus carried our griefs and sorrows. The Hebrew word for *griefs* means 'sicknesses.' The Hebrew word for *sorrows* means 'pains.' Jesus has taken our sicknesses and pains."

I look at the scripture. It's right there in black and white.

"Matthew 8:17 says Jesus fulfilled that promise," Pastor Doc declares.

"Would He heal me? No, I'm not worthy," I say, dismissing the thought.

"Yes, you are," he replies. "Jesus died for you. That makes you worthy."

We look at Isaiah 53:5. "And by His wounds we are healed."

"*Are healed* is not past tense. It's not future tense. It's present tense. We are healed now," he says emphatically. "Do you believe the message?"

I don't answer. I'm speechless.

He presses on, asking, "Does having MS glorify Jesus?"

I stammer, "Well, um, I think so. I tell people Jesus helps me cope with MS."

I'm wriggling in my seat now. He's like a police detective grilling a suspect.

"It's good that you tell people Jesus helps you cope," he says reassuringly.

I know more is coming. He's leaning forward again. Here it comes.

He delivers his final point: "How much greater glory would God receive if you were miraculously healed?"

I'm speechless again. I want to hide somewhere. Of course He would receive greater glory if Jesus healed me.

He isn't like a regular pastor. He challenges rather than comforts. I'm stirred up.

## WRAPPING MY LIFE AROUND JESUS

Pastor Doc prescribes a different kind of medicine than what I'm taking now:

First prescription—"Read and reread the scriptures I'm showing you. Meditate on them, filling your mind with God's truth. Do not empty your mind, like in Eastern religions. That's not what Christianity is about. Fill your mind with the words of Jesus."

Next prescription—"Listen to Christian music from morning to bedtime."

Third prescription—"Pray all the time. Start a conversation with the Father and Jesus."

Expected results—Intimate relationship with God, healing of MS.

Side effects—Righteousness, peace, and joy in the Holy Ghost.

MS is in shock. The Little Helpers stop chewing, horror-stricken.

Pastor Doc prays a compassionate prayer for me to be healed. He's leaving now. He grabs his hat and his gear and he's out the door before I know it.

"See you next week!" he says with a tip of his hat.

I'm hearing truth. I'm stirred up. Jesus' name is above all names, including the name *MS*.

I make my way to the den and announce that Pastor Doc and I are done for the day.

"Would you please order some Christian music CDs?" I ask Jeff. "Pastor Doc says it will be good for me to listen to them all day."

I open the Bible and read the scriptures he assigned. The Word is like hot water. I steep in it like a tea bag. All my tiny little tea leaves absorb it. I'm stirred up again.

Joy floods my heart. I'm overwhelmed. Look at Jesus! Isn't He beautiful? He's altogether lovely. He's altogether mighty. I stand in awe before Him.

Christian music floods the house. I'm bathing in it. Splish, splash! Its sweet fragrance clings to me all day and all night.

MS is far in the background. I'm still very sick, but I don't care. Jesus, I love You! Father, I love You!

I'm wrapping myself around the Lord, entwining myself with Him.

Isaiah 40:31 tells me if I do that, I'll gain new strength and will soar up on wings like an eagle. I'll run and not grow tired, walk and not grow weary.

It hasn't happened yet, but it will. I know it will. God says so, right here in black and white, and in red, too. Those are Jesus' words.

# Chapter Ten

# THE WORD IS A SWORD

**P**ASTOR DOC IS back for another visit.

Incredulous, I say, "Satan exists? You've got to be kidding, Doc."

"Jesus isn't talking to Himself in the wilderness," he says, as we look at Matthew 4.

"Oh, yeah. You're right about that one," I say, embarrassed again.

We look at Daniel 10 next. Daniel's answer from God was blocked for twenty-one days by a demon. One of the chief princes, Michael, helped the messenger get through. It appears to have happened somewhere between heaven and here. There's a realm I didn't know about. The devil and his demons are real and at work.

"You're catching on quickly," Pastor Doc says. "If the devil can block a message to Daniel, can he do the same to you?"

"Yup, and Daniel was esteemed by God. I don't think I am. Satan can really take a shot at me. I have no defense," I reply.

Pastor Doc takes me to Hebrews 4:12 (NIV): "For the word of God is living and active. Sharper than any double-edged sword, it penetrates even to dividing soul and spirit, joints and marrow; it judges the thoughts and attitudes of the heart."

He says, "The Word is a sword against Satan. We can use it like Jesus did when Satan tempted Him in the wilderness."

I exclaim, "Let's get that Word into me, so I can fight MS and Satan!"

MS is terror-stricken. Sprawled out on its corner stool, it looks at me, wild-eyed. *What on earth is she doing?*

I'm worshiping the Lord. Earth has nothing to do with it.

My heart soars as I read the Word. Take that, Satan. Hush up, MS. Quit your munching, Little Helpers.

## Confusing the Enemy

Pastor Doc says, "Worship the Lord, and He'll confuse the enemy."

Second Chronicles 20 says King Jehoshaphat's small army faced a vast army of Judah's enemies. He cried out to the Lord. A prophet of the Lord answered: "The battle belongs to the Lord." Jehoshaphat would be victorious because the Lord was fighting the battle. When his army heard the news, everyone rejoiced and worshiped.

Jehoshaphat sent the unarmed Levites, chosen by God to lead worship, out ahead of his army. The Levites went forth, singing and praising God. The Lord ambushed the enemy armies and confused them. The result? They killed each other off. Jehoshaphat's army never even had to raise a sword. The enemy armies were already dead by the time his army reached their camps.

"I like that! I'll worship all the more," I say. "Thanks, Pastor Doc."

Worshiping the Lord with song, the Word and prayer breaks down Satan's strongholds. He flees in confusion.

MS is mortified. The connoisseurs of my central nervous system gasp in horror. Half-eaten nerve sheaths fall out of their open mouths.

## Worship Connects Me to God

External worship becomes internal. At first I mechanically took my worship prescription. Now I am living and breathing worship with every breath. It is life, it is joy! I can hardly wait to get up in the morning. Fatigue? Who cares? Tremor? Nothing can stop me. I have an appointment with my Father!

Oh, Jesus, I see Your face. You are altogether lovely. I can't take my eyes off You!

I'm stirred up when Pastor Doc comes. The feeling fades when he leaves. I read the Word of God, worship with music and pray. I'm stirred up again. Worship connects me to God.

Oh, Lord, I am tasting You and seeing that You are good. I love You! I feel Your strength come in as I wrap myself around You.

## MY TURN TO PRAY

On the third visit, Pastor Doc says, "I usually pray at the end of our sessions, but this time, I want you to pray."

"What will I pray?" I ask.

"Why don't you tell God exactly what needs to happen in your body in order for you to be healed?" he asks.

I know the facts, from the clinical scene. Now I get clinical, in Jesus' name. He's greater than my disease.

Lord, my blood-brain barrier is compromised. My brain is under attack by my body's own immune system. Insulation is stripped off the nerves in my brain, spinal cord and optic nerves.

*Stop!* cries MS.

*She knows too much!* the Little Helpers cry frantically.

Be quiet. I'm praying. No interruptions allowed.

Lord, heal the lesions MS has created. Make my brain the way it was before MS. I'm handing it over to You, Lord. Help me.

I unscrew the top of my head, tip it to the side, tap gently, and watch all of man's wisdom fall out. There, I've pitched it all. Now, what do You say, Lord?

Jesus replies, "All things are possible to him who believes," (Mark 9:23).

I believe the message, Lord.

## THANKING GOD

Pastor Doc says, "You need to thank God for what He's doing in you, and what He's going to do."

I'm ready. That night, I pray to the Father:

*Thank You. I know Jesus is going to heal me.*

47

*Thank You for loving me so much that You sent Him to die on a cross for my sin.*

*Thank You that because I believe in Jesus, You have forgiven me for rebelling against You all those years.*

*Thank You for eternal life that starts here and now.*

*Thank You, Jesus, for loving and obeying the Father. Thank You for saving the likes of me. You gave up all Your glory to do it.*

*Thank You, God, for Your life-giving Word. It is sweeter than honey from the comb.*

I thank God continuously.

# Chapter Eleven

## AND THE WINNER IS...

YOU'VE SHOWED ME the Word of God, Jesus. I'm focused on you now. I know You will heal me.

MS rustles. *Pssst, Satan! Come in like a flood and overwhelm her.*

The Little Helpers chime in, *Yeah. We want to keep our jobs.*

On the night of September 1, 2001, Jeff and I are ready for some much-needed sleep. As I lie in bed, I stretch my spastic legs and try to untie my hopelessly knotted neck and shoulder muscles. After I've done the best I can with them, I lay my jerking head on the pillow, waiting for the tremors to ease so that I can drop off to sleep. I turn out the light.

Satan whispers, *Who do you think you are? You're not worthy to be healed. Besides, MS is incurable. Your tremors are irreversible. Healing isn't for today. You're fooling yourself.*

I'm overwhelmed. An unexpected wave just washed over me, and I'm drowning. Where did that come from?

I sob convulsively on Jeff's shoulder. At least with MS, I knew what my future was. Now I've stuck my neck out and I don't know what will happen.

Jeff comforts me, holding me close. He doesn't know what to say. I eventually calm down a bit. He releases me, wearily rolls over and falls asleep.

I lie in the darkened bedroom, staring up at the ceiling. I'm desolate. I blew it. Forgive me, Lord. I've let you down by not believing You. Where is my faith?

Suddenly, I remember Peter walking on the water toward Jesus.

He was doing fine until he looked at the stormy sea. Then he started sinking.

He cried out to Jesus, "Lord! Save me!"

Jesus took hold of him and lifted him to safety.

"You of little faith, why did you doubt?" He said.

I'm in a storm, too, looking at the raging sea instead of Jesus.

"You're sinking in a sea of doubt," Jesus says to my heart.

I know it's true. With faith the size of a tiny mustard seed, I reach up in the night just like Peter did in Matthew 14:31.

"Help me, Jesus!" I cry.

Immediately, I sense that He's lifting me out of my sea of doubt. I must get up so I can be with the Lord in His Word. I'm more stirred up than ever before.

## ANOINTED HEAD TO TOE

I sit with the Word on my lap. It is so good! I love to be in it, hearing Jesus' voice. I hear Him more clearly than ever tonight. Midnight comes and September 2, 2001 arrives.

Wow! What's happening? I suddenly feel a tingling sensation.

MS flees my body. Sprawled out on the canvas, it's down for the final count.

The tingling sensation continues. It's like oil trickling down from my head to my feet, but inside of me instead of on my skin. Head to toe, Jesus anoints me.

I know I'm healed! Hallelujah!

The referee holds up my hand. "And the winner is... Jesus!"

I'm the recipient of Jesus Christ's victory. His life surges through my veins. I worship Him, rejoicing, praising Him and praying.

O Lord, You did it! I was "Sue of little faith," but like Peter, I cried out to You with my tiny bit of faith. You rescued me from the sea of doubt and healed my body!

After a couple of hours, I rise from the couch to go to bed. Strength comes through my whole body! I lie down, overwhelmed with joy indescribable and full of glory.

Morning arrives. Fatigue is no longer my companion. The

tremors are gone. I've been plugged into a super-sized recharger all night. The power is from God, given by the Holy Spirit.

## WALKING AND LEAPING AND PRAISING GOD

Acts 3 says the beggar at Gate Beautiful wanted money from Peter and John. His attention was on his hopeless condition. He cried out for alms.

Peter said, "Look at us! I don't have silver and gold for you, but in the name of Jesus Christ of Nazareth, walk!"

The beggar had never walked in his life. Peter grabbed the beggar's hand. The man stood up. He was so overjoyed that he couldn't stop walking and leaping and praising God.

That's me, even all these years later. I walk and leap and praise God! I walk with Jesus by faith. I leap for joy. I praise God for His mercy toward such a one as me.

The third verse of the hymn "And Can It Be" comes to my mind:

Long my imprisoned spirit lay,
Fast bound in sin and nature's night;
Thine eye diffused a quick'ning ray—
I woke, the dungeon flamed with light;
My chains fell off, my heart was free,
I rose, went forth, and followed Thee.
—CHARLES WESLEY, 1738

The prisoner is free! The bound one is released! Light from God's very eye invaded my MS dungeon. It flamed with His light. My chains of sickness fell off.

Oh, glory! I rise and go forth to follow Jesus. How could I do anything else?

# Chapter Twelve

# THE GIFT OF FAITH

L ATER ON THAT day, the Lord says, "It's all right to stop your medications now."

I make plans to taper off all my pills. Every step is a step of faith, from the moment I was healed. I reserve enough pills for the tapering process.

Jeff is awake now. He's on the La-Z-Boy, reading the newspaper. I vigorously walk by, carrying a trash bag full of pill bottles. He hears the bag rattle its way into the trash. He watches me throw away the Copaxone that was in the refrigerator.

"What are you doing?" Jeff asks, puzzled and quite concerned.

I joyfully announce, "Jesus healed me!"

Faith flows into Jeff. From that moment on, he never doubts my healing.

Later, someone asks him, "What will you do when Sue crashes?"

Jeff says, "Why don't you ask Sue? She's not crashing, anyway. She's healed by Jesus!"

I have no symptoms as I gradually stop each medication. O Lord, You did it!

## THE GOD OF MORE THAN ENOUGH

He is the God of more than enough. He heals me of carpal tunnel, allergies and asthma as well as MS.

Jesus, I only asked You to heal me of MS. You're supplying much more.

I see the loaves and fishes multiplied. Prayers are more than answered by Jesus.

I call Mom. Jesus healed me in the middle of the night! She rejoices.

Hi, bro! Jesus healed me!

"That's wonderful," he says. "But you should go to the doctor for blood tests. Maybe they can detect what's in your blood that caused your healing. It might help others."

There's no blood test for Jesus, but I'm glad to share Him.

## MY FAITH IS TESTED

Stopping Neurontin is hard. It muffled my tremors a bit. Though I haven't had a tremor since the night Jesus healed me, I'm terrified that they might return. O me of little faith!

I cry out, "Lord, help my unbelief!"

He increases my faith. I begin tapering but there are withdrawal symptoms.

I visit Nice-clinical and tell him I believe Jesus has healed me but I'm having a hard time withdrawing from Neurontin. He doesn't question me.

He says, "I'll draw up a schedule for you to taper off. Just ride out the withdrawal symptoms."

There are still no tremors after I'm completely off Neurontin. Jesus has recreated nerve cells in my brain. Nerves chomped in two are now made new!

He has healed me for His name's sake and for His glory. His Miracle-Worker reputation is at stake. He shows Himself to be faithful and never goes back on His Word.

Physically healed, I remember that the most important healing took place when I was reconciled to God by believing Jesus Christ is my Lord and Savior. All glory to You, Father, Son, and Holy Spirit!

The Lord's healing power continues to work in me. In November 2001, I'm watching TV with my glasses perched on my nose, as usual. Suddenly, my vision blurs. I panic briefly. Is this optic neuritis? What if I was wrong about being healed?

Then I hear the Lord say to my heart, "Try a weaker prescription."

I have many pairs of glasses in my nightstand, evidence of the

Little Helpers gnawing on my optic nerves all those years. Every bite meant a stronger prescription.

I try on my next oldest prescription. My vision is less blurry. I try on the next and the next and the next. My vision is clearer and clearer and clearer! I don the glasses I wore before I was stricken in 1996. They're just right for me.

I laugh and cry, "Oh, Lord, You're so kind to me!"

# Chapter Thirteen

# THE HEALING IS INVESTIGATED

I'M COMPELLED TO shout from the rooftops! We call the *Kennebec Journal* in Augusta, Maine, to see if they'll publish our testimony of Jesus. The reporter interviews Jeff and me and takes his article to the editorial board. Will they publish?

The editor says, "No way. MS is incurable."

We dig out the Brigham and Women's tape and find the spot where Research-clinical says, "You have axonal burnout. The tremors are irreversible."

The reporter takes the tape to the editorial board. I obviously don't have tremors now. The editor relents. "MS Victim Lives Easter" is published March 23, 2002.

The state's Christian paper, the *Good News Connection*, spreads our good news, too. Jesus, You whispered to us and we're shouting!

## NICE-CLINICAL EXAMINES ME

Pastor Doc says, "You should go back to your neurologist again. You'll need more proof of the healing. People will doubt."

I set up an appointment with Nice-clinical. I feel fine.

Satan whispers, *What if the doctor finds something you can't feel?*

I fight him with the Word. I know that He who is in me is greater than he who is in the world, just as it says in 1 John 4:4. The truth of that scripture has been permanently planted in my heart.

Sitting alone on the bedroom floor, I pray for Jesus to give me more faith. I submit to God and resist the devil. Satan has to flee. It's the law, just like it says in James 4:7.

On April 16, 2002, I glide effortlessly into the office, Jeff at my side. I glow and grin. Nice-clinical is astonished. "Sue! You're not the same woman I saw a few months ago! What has happened?"

"Oh, Nice-clinical, I am so much more than healed of MS. But give me a neurological exam, please," I joyfully reply.

He is an ophthalmologist as well as a neurologist. He begins with my left eye. He knows I have "scarring" on my left optic disc from optic neuritis. The scarring has disappeared.

Flabbergasted, he exclaims, "This is God!"

I share my testimony as he examines the rest of me. The neurological exam is completely normal. He gives me a clean bill of health.

"Have a nice life," he says as we leave the office.

We will, Nice-clinical. Jesus lives in our hearts!

His progress note says:

> Through her church, Sue's been healed. Her MS is healed. Her CTS [carpal tunnel syndrome] symptoms cleared. Going into ordination program—preparing to start that in Sept. Has given sermons, testimonials, etc.—most recently in Schroon Lake, NY.

Compare that with the notes from the initial visit on October 22, 1998:

> Motor examination shows a wide-based ataxic gait with right leg weaker than left. Muscle bulk is normal. Tone is increased in both lower extremities...The patient has an affirmative tremor of the head which fluctuates in intensity during the examination and seems to diminish somewhat with distraction. Toes are downgoing. Impression: Question primary progressive multiple sclerosis versus secondary progressive multiple sclerosis.

Oh, praise Jesus, You are the Healer! With God, all things are possible!

# EYE DOCTOR EXAMINES ME

It's time for my regular eye exam with Eye-clinical, two years later. As she examines my left eye, she looks puzzled. I remember that I haven't told her I'm healed.

"The scarring is gone on my left optic nerve, isn't it?" I ask.

She slowly says, "Yesss…"

I give her my testimony. The rest of the exam is normal.

In October 2008, I ask Eye-clinical if I can use her name in a book I'm writing.

She says, "We have to be careful about these things. I can certainly report that you had a sudden improvement in your vision. Your left optic disc seems a little pale to me, though. Will you allow me to do a visual field exam? If it's normal, you can use my name."

I pray. Jesus, show her what You did.

He does. Both eyes see 95 percent of the flashing lights in the exam. She says there's no longer any evidence of functional damage in my left eye, though she declines to allow me to use her name.

# Chapter Fourteen

# JOY INEXPRESSIBLE

"THERE'S MORE I want to do in you," Jesus says.

But this life is already wonderful, Lord.

Just before I was healed, Pastor Doc gave me a book called *Ever Increasing Faith*, by Smith Wigglesworth. I learned that if I'm filled with the Holy Spirit, I will have power to testify about the Lord. I checked it out in the Word and found that it's true.

I've had a taste of You, Lord. I want all of You. Fill me with Your Spirit so I can be Your witness. I need Your power in order to give my testimony of You.

Oh, I can know the Father and Jesus more! Hallelujah! Full surrender of my will to God's will is required. I surrender all. The way is prepared for heaven to open in my soul.

## FILLED WITH THE SPIRIT!

It's November 1, 2001. I get a call from our Spirit-filled neighbor, Jenny Bailey. She's been an encourager from the time I began to seek the Lord.

"I was in prayer," she says, "and the Lord asked me to call you. Do you want to be baptized in the Holy Spirit?"

"I'll be right over," I say, and quickly hang up the telephone.

Calling over my shoulder as I dash to the door, I say, "Jeff, I'm going to Jenny's. Be back soon."

Jenny and I read Scripture. She explains that Jesus baptizes in the Holy Spirit. We pray. Her usually rambunctious daughter sits peacefully in her little chair, watching us.

Suddenly, I shake all over. I'm baptized in the Holy Spirit, filled with joy. I speak in a strange language, but I know I'm saying, "Father mine, Father mine!"

Jenny says, "You've just spoken in tongues."

God's love fills me, His Spirit fills me, my sin nature dies and Christ's nature comes in. No longer fast bound in sin and nature's night, I'm free!

I come home glowing.

Jeff says, "What happened to you?"

I announce, "I've been filled with the Holy Spirit!"

He panics. "Sue is going on with You, Lord. Show me how to be filled," he prays. "because I want to go on with You, too."

I'm flooded with joy beyond description. It bubbles over, spilling out. I'm laughing softly in the Spirit.

I take a walk through the neighborhood, speaking in tongues as I leap and jump for joy. I notice that I'm able to understand what I'm saying.

"You have the gift of interpretation," Pastor Doc later explains.

I don't know anything about spiritual gifts. The Spirit gives them anyway.

As I open the Word of God, heavenly light shines on it. I suddenly have a deep understanding of it. The Author leads me now; He lives in me. The Holy Spirit continues to reveal more and more of God to me, and will for the rest of my life.

## A PURE HEART

When I walk through the door after the experience at Jenny's, the house looks the same, but something's not quite right. Oh, now I see. I'm looking at everything around me through Jesus' eyes.

CDs, magazines, and books fly into the trash. I should pay my trash collector double for the next few weeks.

I'm cleansed, my heart purified and prepared to do His will! Thank You, Lord! I love You with Your love. It has filled my heart!

What about the things of this world? They mean nothing. I want heavenly things. I want what God wants. My heart is all love for Him.

"Whom have I in heaven but You? And besides You, I desire nothing on earth." That's Psalm 73:25. I sing it with the psalmist.

My heart is Yours, O God, offered to You in flames of holy love. Oh, joy inexpressible and full of glory!

But Jesus, I'm not completely like You yet.

"Don't worry, child," He says to my heart. "We will mold and shape you into My image."

It's a lifetime project. I love every moment of it. There's nothing about me that I treasure. I just want to be more like Him.

Change me, Lord, from glory to glory, from image to image, by Your Spirit! I strive to lay hold of that for which You have laid hold of me.

Oh, to be like Christ! Continuing transformation, love, holy desire, joy, and peace. Oh, it is glorious!

## JEFF FILLED WITH THE SPIRIT!

Jeff seeks the Spirit, praying and wrestling for eight days after I'm filled.

Pastor Doc comes. We sit at the table, steaming mugs of coffee in our hands. Those piercing blue eyes search Jeff.

He says, "Jeff, you look awful!"

"I feel awful!" Jeff exclaims. Doc frowns slightly.

Jeff continues, "I want to be filled with the Holy Spirit. I've prayed, surrendered everything and asked forgiveness for every sin. I even surrendered Sue to Him."

Pastor Doc says, "Are you sure you've repented for everything?"

"Everything! Even dreams I may have had, sins I can't remember." Jeff is desperate.

Pastor Doc stands up, moves behind Jeff, lays his hands on Jeff's shoulders and speaks a few words in tongues.

The Holy Spirit fills Jeff! He raises his hands in praise. His face is like an angel's. Hallelujah!

After watching him for a while, Pastor Doc and I move to the living room to worship. We leave Jeff in God's hands. Jeff wanders into the living room nearly two hours later, glowing with the Lord's presence. Glory!

# SERVING CHRIST TOGETHER

Jeff and I are one now, partners in serving God. We love each other with His love. We love Him with His love. Oh, what a gift! Christ reigns in both of us!

Our unity is on a level we never could have imagined; He ensures that our gifts dovetail. He prepares us to share Him with others. We have Christ's mind. Power flows in and through us to proclaim, heal and set the captives free. Christ works through us. Our marriage becomes a picture of Christ and His church. Our only desire is to allow Him to mold and shape us into His image. We don't resist His loving hands.

Psalm 37:4 reads, "Delight yourself in the LORD, and He will give you the desires of your heart." O Lord, I have made myself pliable in Your hands. Now Your desires are my desires. I live for You. Be glorified!

# Chapter Fifteen

## LEARNING TO BE SPIRIT-LED

WHAT DO YOU want me to do, Lord? I pray and fast. I only want to do what You want to do. Should I return to my job at the VA?

A big *no* appears in my heart.

Amen, Lord, so be it. Retirement, health insurance and other benefits mean nothing to me now. Jeff understands. He delights to do God's will, too.

I write to the Medicare people and to the Office of Personnel Management (OPM). I'm not sick anymore. Cancel my benefits.

The phone rings a few days later. It's M_ from OPM. She's not used to having someone write to cancel disability benefits. "What do you want us to do, ma'am?" she drawls, "Your file is in the dead file."

"I'm not dead anymore, but alive and well and living with Jesus in my heart," I joyfully respond.

She understands and rejoices with me, sharing the news with others in her office.

God is teaching me to hear from Him. He says He has a different plan for me. I don't know what it is, but I know He's going to show me.

Nice-clinical sends his findings to the OPM on the appropriate form. They write back to me, "Based upon the information you provided, we have determined that you are no longer entitled for disability retirement payments...Please notify us if you accept a position within the Federal government."

I've accepted a position in the kingdom of God. He says He wants to make me useable there.

# NEON SIGNS NEEDED

Lord, I need neon signs that flash, "Sue, this is the way!"

I don't know anything about following You, but I'll dance down the path as You light my way. I'll go anywhere with You.

Show me open doors and I'll go through them. What you open, no man can shut. That's what You say in Isaiah 22:22.

# POETRY AND MUSIC

Poetry from the Lord flows from my prose-only pen. By January 2002, the poems have turned into songs. Melodies and lyrics are downloaded from heaven to my heart. I smile as I remember the song He gave me in 2000. It was a preview of things to come.

Jeff and I look for neon signs. Richard "Stonefingers" Johnson comes to our church. He ministers with music and the Word in prisons across the country.

Maybe this is what we're supposed to do. The Lord sent Stonefingers to us as a sign.

"Pastor Doc, we think we're supposed to start a music ministry soon," we say.

"No, not yet," he says with a note of fatherly concern in his voice. "It's too soon. You're not ready."

We obey him. He's our leader and we're all disciples of Jesus.

Seven years later, we minister at the Maine State Prison as well as at a church. Our timing was a bit off, Lord. You just smile, knowing our hearts are filled with Your love.

# ANOINTED TO PREACH AND TEACH

In January 2002, Pastor Doc says, "I'm going to be away at a conference. Sue, I want you to preach while I'm gone. I want the flock to hear the difference in you."

I'm not sure what he means by "the difference." The congregation heard me preach corporate trainer-style a couple of times before Pastor Doc came to our church.

He gives me the Scripture he wants me to use. I pray and study diligently.

It's Sunday morning. I open my Bible and open my mouth. The power of God flows through me. His words come forth, for His glory.

When Pastor Doc returns, he listens to the recording of the sermon.

"You have an anointing for preaching," he remarks.

He comes to me again, a few weeks later. "We need a teacher for a Bible study. I think you should try it."

I'm a bit awkward at first but then get into His stride.

Pastor Doc says, "You have a teaching anointing. Jeff and you should think about becoming pastors."

We are presented to the church board. They agree we have pastoral potential. We begin the journey toward ordination, taking courses in theology, church history, inductive Bible study, pastoral care and so on.

Pastor Doc graciously gives us time in the pulpit.

## HEALING HANDS

Jeff hears from the Lord after he's filled with the Spirit.

The Lord says, "You have healing hands." He tells Pastor Doc.

At an evening church service, Pastor Doc says, "Jeff, please go and lay hands on S_ and pray for her to be healed. She has a cold."

Jeff steps out in faith, obedient to the Lord's calling. S_'s cold is gone the next morning.

Debbie and John are with us at a church supper. Debbie is allergic to oranges. She unwittingly drinks some punch that contains orange juice. She has an allergic reaction, coughing and itching, eyes watering. Jeff lays hands on her and prays for the Lord to heal her. The allergic reaction instantly stops.

Repeatedly, Jeff's hands are used by the Lord to heal.

I'm about to leave for a spiritual retreat. I've been invited to share how Jesus healed me. Jeff, Pastor Doc and I stand in the kitchen with our hands linked, praying.

Pastor Doc says, "Sue, if you have a chance to lay hands on anyone for healing, do it."

I'm at the retreat now. A woman is having an asthma attack. I see her use her inhaler and figure she'll be all right in a few minutes. I wrestled with asthma before the Lord healed me.

Later, she's sprawled out in a chair with women praying all around her. Her lips have turned blue. Jesus propels me out of my chair. On my way to her, I begin to weep. It's His compassion flowing into my heart and out my eyes.

I sit beside her and begin to pray out loud, "Jesus, I don't know what to do, but You do."

I ask her if I can lay my right hand on her upper chest.

She gasps, "Yes."

A minute or two later, she's breathing normally. She smiles. I continue to keep my hand on her chest until she begins to laugh gently. Then I know it's done.

The next day, beaming, she says, "I still feel your hand on my chest!"

That's not my hand. It's His. I grin broadly and she shines back at me.

Another woman approaches me at the retreat. She's a stranger to me.

"God just told me that if I tell my problems to you, you'll have the answer," she says confidently.

I listen to her story. Her problems seem beyond repair. I don't know what to say. Help me, Lord Jesus!

She finishes and looks at me expectantly. I open my mouth. The words bring her to repentance and tears. She is healed. Thank You, Lord.

He has filled me with His Spirit so I may bring good news to the afflicted, bind up the brokenhearted and set the captives free. I must, you know. I'm compelled by the love of God. Jesus commands me in Matthew 10:8: "Heal the sick, raise the dead, cleanse the lepers, cast out demons. Freely you received, freely give." Just as You command, Lord.

# Chapter Sixteen

# THIS LIFE, YOUR LIFE

L IVING WITH JESUS in my heart is glorious. Being set free from Satan's clutches and the power of sin is freedom beyond words. Being filled with the love of God and His blessed Holy Spirit is indescribably powerful. Being a daughter of my Father in heaven is joy inexpressible and full of glory. Life before Jesus was mere existence. He healed much more than my body.

Why did He heal me? So that I may proclaim the excellencies of Him who brought me out of darkness into His marvelous light. My disease was beyond man's ability to cure, and yet I am healed, brought into His divine life, and filled with His love.

## WHAT HE WANTS TO DO IN YOUR HEART

The Father loves you so much He sent His Son, Jesus, to die for you, to pay what you owe God for your sin. You've rebelled against Him. Jesus is God's gift to you. Gifts are meant to be received and opened. Open Him!

Jesus Christ loves you so much He died on a cross for you. Believe in Him, enter His life and be forgiven for your sins.

He has presented Himself to you as you have read my account of His work in my life. He really is God the Son. No one but God could heal me. Jesus Christ is not just an idea in someone's head or a good example to follow. He is real. That means the Bible is true, and you need Him.

All have sinned and lack the glory of God (see Romans 3:23). Your rebellion against God is like a yoke on your neck. It's your ticket to hell. In Matthew 11:28–30, Jesus announces His cure for your condition:

> Come to Me, all who are weary and heavy-laden, and I will give you rest. Take My yoke upon you and learn from Me, for I am gentle and humble in heart, and you will find rest for your souls. For My yoke is easy and My burden is light.

Come to Him!

As for me, my journey with Him is just beginning, and it has no end!

# Appendix A

# SCRIPTURE PRESCRIPTIONS

Pastor Doc is a good teacher. He took me through my paces. I'm sharing with you some of the scriptures he prescribed, praying that the Lord touches you through them. May He heal your heart and your body and fill you with His love.

## THE ARMOR OF GOD

### Ephesians 6:14–18 (NIV)

> Stand firm, then, with the belt of truth buckled around your waist, with the breastplate of righteousness in place, and with your feet fitted with the readiness that comes from the gospel of peace. In addition to all this, take up the shield of faith, with which you can extinguish all the flaming arrows of the evil one. Take the helmet of salvation and the sword of the Spirit, which is the word of God. And pray in the Spirit on all occasions, with all kinds of prayers and requests. With this in mind, be alert and always keep on praying for all the saints.

Do you believe in Jesus Christ? Does He dwell in your heart? Then put on God's armor every day, in preparation for Satan's attacks. God's armor covers you entirely so that when Satan looks at you, he will only be able to see His armor, not you. And God also promises to be your rear guard (see Isaiah 52:12), so you know by faith that there is no part of you that Satan can successfully attack. And pray, pray, pray.

# VICTORY IN JESUS

### 1 John 4:4 (NIV)

> You, dear children, are from God and have overcome them, because the one who is in you is greater than the one who is in the world.

Do you believe Jesus is the Son of God? Then Jesus is in you. The devil is "the one who is in the world." Jesus came to destroy the works of the devil (1 John 3:8). Jesus in you defeats Satan every time.

### James 4:7 (NIV)

> Submit yourselves, then, to God. Resist the devil, and he will flee from you.

You have faith in God and Christ. You are reading His Word. You are obeying Him. You are worshiping Him. If these things are true, then the devil has to flee. You're submitting to God!

### Hebrews 11:1

> Now faith is the assurance of things hoped for, the conviction of things not seen.

*Your situation is hopeless*, Satan whispers in your ear. If Jesus dwells in your heart, you have faith. You don't need to see the results yet. You just know and trust your Father and His Son, no matter how bad things look.

### Isaiah 40:31

> Yet those who wait for the LORD will gain new strength; they will mount up with wings like eagles, they will run and not get tired, they will walk and not become weary.

This promise is for those whose hearts have Jesus in them. The word "wait" means "entwine yourself with." Wrap yourself around the Lord. You'll gain His strength.

**2 Corinthians 10:5 (NIV)**

> We demolish arguments and every pretension that sets itself
> up against the knowledge of God, and we take captive every
> thought to make it obedient to Christ.

Do you know Jesus personally? Do you sometimes doubt His
ability to help you? Demolish those arguments against God. Take
captive every thought. Obey Christ's teachings. Believe Him.

**Isaiah 53:5 (NIV)**

> But He was pierced for our transgressions, He was crushed
> for our iniquities; the punishment that brought us peace was
> upon Him, and by His wounds we are healed.

Have you been born from above into the kingdom of God?
No? The good news is that Jesus died to take away all the bad
things you've done. He's also come to give you an obedient heart,
and to heal your physical body, just like it says in Isaiah 53:4 and
Matthew 8:17. He took up our infirmities and carried our diseases.

**Hebrews 13:8**

> Jesus Christ is the same yesterday and today and forever.

There are no time limits on Jesus' work. He is still saving, deliv-
ering, and healing.

**1 John 5:4–5 (AMP)**

> For whatever is born of God is victorious over the world; and
> this is the victory that conquers the world, even our faith.
> Who is it that is victorious [that conquers] the world but he
> who believes that Jesus is the Son of God [who adheres to,
> trusts in, and relies on that fact]?

If you are born of God, you believe Jesus is the Son of God. God
gave you that faith. Now, walk in His victory. You are more than a
conqueror through Him who loves you (see Romans 8:37).

## Psalm 91 (NIV)

Read it and believe it. Remember that to dwell in the shelter of the Most High, you must be united to Him in love and settled down with Him like in a marriage. If this describes you, Psalm 91's promises are yours. If not, ask God to forgive you and change your heart. He will.

## Psalm 107:19–20

> Then they cried out to the LORD in their trouble; He saved them out of their distresses. He sent His word and healed them, and delivered them from their destructions.

The Word heals in every way. He's wonderful. It's wonderful. Read it!

# SEEK GOD

## Matthew 6:33

> But seek first His kingdom and His righteousness, and all these things will be added to you.

When you seek first the kingdom of God, allowing Him to sit on the throne in your heart, you are covered with Christ's righteousness, and the Father's hand will provide what you need.

## James 4:8 (NIV)

> Come near to God and He will come near to you.

Are you far from God? Then draw near. He'll draw near to you. You were created to have intimate fellowship with Him. That's His design and plan. Do what I did. Rejoice evermore!

# Healing, a Benefit of God

**Psalm 103:2–5**

> Bless the Lord, O my soul, and forget none of His benefits;
> Who pardons all your iniquities, Who heals all your dis-
> eases; Who redeems your life from the pit, Who crowns you
> with lovingkindness and compassion; Who satisfies your
> years with good things, So that your youth is renewed like
> the eagle.

The original Hebrew word for "diseases" is *tachalu*. It liter-
ally means "sicknesses, maladies." Two of His benefits are in view
here—forgiveness of sin and physical healing. That is what Jesus
Christ did when He walked the earth, and what He still does today.
Want to be healed? First seek forgiveness for your sins and forgive
others who have sinned against you. Then believe His promises
are yours.

# God's Will

**John 5:19**

> Therefore Jesus answered and was saying to them, "Truly,
> truly, I say to you, the Son can do nothing of Himself, unless
> it is something He sees the Father doing; for whatever the
> Father does, these things the Son also does in like manner."

Jesus sees the Father heal. Jesus heals. Jesus sees the Father
deliver. Jesus delivers. It's God's nature.

**1 John 5:14–15**

> This is the confidence which we have before Him, that, if we
> ask anything according to His will, He hears us. And if we
> know that He hears us in whatever we ask, we know that we
> have the requests which we have asked from Him.

God will not answer your demands, but He will answer your heartfelt, humble prayer. When you ask, don't doubt. He'll do it, if your heart is right before Him.

### John 10:10

> The thief comes only to steal and kill and destroy; I came that they may have life, and have it abundantly.

God's will is to put Christ's abundant life into your heart, so you can become like Jesus. Ask Him to live and reign in your heart. He'll take care of the rest. Trust Him.

### Matthew 8:16

> When evening came, they brought to Him many who were demon-possessed; and He cast out the spirits with a word, and healed all who were ill.

Jesus healed each one.

### Matthew 12:15b (NIV)

> Aware of this [that the Pharisees sought to destroy Him], Jesus withdrew from that place. Many followed Him, and He healed them all.

Jesus excluded no one.

### Matthew 8:2–3 (NIV)

> A man with leprosy came and knelt before Him and said, "Lord, if you are willing, you can make me clean." Jesus reached out His hand and touched the man. "I am willing," He said. "Be clean!"

The Lord is willing to cleanse and heal you.

**Matthew 10:1 (NIV)**

> He called His twelve disciples to Him, and gave them
> authority to drive out evil spirits and to heal every disease
> and sickness.

His name is above everything. Only the Father is greater than
Jesus (John 14:28). Nothing can stand up against Jesus. Do you
believe the message?

**Isaiah 53:1 (NIV)**

> Who has believed our message and to whom has the arm of
> the LORD been revealed?

The strength of the Lord is revealed to those who believe.
Matthew 8:16–17 confirms it: "When evening came, many who
were demon-possessed were brought to Him [by people who
believed He could help them], and He drove out the spirits with a
word and healed all the sick. This was to fulfill what was spoken
through the prophet Isaiah: 'He took up our infirmities, and carried our diseases.'" Christ heals in every way.

## FAITH

**Hebrews 11**

Read it and meditate upon it. Then walk in faith because you
know God is faithful.

**Matthew 8:10**

> Now when Jesus heard this, He marveled and said to those
> who were following, "Truly I say to you, I have not found
> such great faith with anyone in Israel."

The centurion has unwavering faith that Jesus can heal his servant without Christ ever touching the servant!

## Mark 9:22–24 (NIV)

A man brought his epileptic son to the disciples, who were unable to heal the child. The man saw Jesus returning from the Mount of Transfiguration, and said:

> But if You can do anything, take pity on us and help us. "'If you can'?" said Jesus. "Everything is possible for him who believes." Immediately the boy's father exclaimed, "I do believe; help me overcome my unbelief!"

Have you reached the end of your faith? Cry out, "I do believe; help me overcome my unbelief!" He will.

## Matthew 15:28

> Then Jesus said to her, "O woman, your faith is great; it shall be done for you as you wish." And her daughter was healed at once.

The Canaanite woman bravely asked for mercy from Jesus for her demon-possessed daughter.

## Matthew 9:28–30

Two blind men approached. "Do you believe that I am able to do this?" Jesus asked. They said to Him, "Yes, Lord." "Then He touched their eyes, saying, 'It shall be done to you according to your faith,'" and their sight was restored. They had faith that He was able to make them see, and they were healed according to their faith.

# REPENTANCE

## Matthew 4:17 (NIV)

> From that time on Jesus began to preach, "Repent, for the kingdom of heaven is near!"

To repent means to have a change of heart and attitude, turning away from sin and toward God. In Mark 1, Jesus proclaims the kingdom of God, saying, "Repent! For the kingdom of God is near!" Indeed it is! If you turn to God, and seek Him, He will set up His kingdom in your heart. Then He will rule and reign, and you will rejoice evermore, here on earth and later, in His kingdom in heaven.

## Sins Forgiven

**Matthew 2:5, 11 (NIV)**

> A paralytic was lowered through the roof, to where Jesus was teaching. When Jesus saw their faith, He said to the paralytic, "Son, your sins are forgiven...get up, take your mat and go home."

First the man's sins were forgiven; then he was healed.

## Man Born Blind, But Had Not Sinned

**John 9:1–41 (NIV)**

> "Neither this man nor his parents sinned," said Jesus, "but this happened so that the work of God might be displayed in his life" (v. 3).

Sin wasn't the issue with this man. He was born blind so he could be miraculously healed by Jesus Christ.

## Worship

**2 Chronicles 20:21–24**

Worship confuses the enemy. Read the account. The enemy armies destroy each other when Jehoshaphat sends out worshipers ahead of his army. Worship God. He will confuse Satan and his demons.

**John 9:31 (AMP)**

> We know that God does not listen to sinners; but if anyone is God-fearing and a worshiper of Him and does His will, He listens to him.

God does not listen to sinners. Turn away from your sin, ask God to forgive you, and then worship the Lord with every breath you take.

## WORSHIP/REVELATION OF CHRIST AS THE SON OF GOD

**John 9:38**

> And he said "Lord, I believe." And he worshiped Him.

This man would never have worshiped a mere human; he had a revelation that Jesus Christ was God in the flesh, the Son of God.

**Matthew 8:2**

> And a leper came to Him and bowed down before Him, and said, "Lord, if you are willing, You can make me clean."

The original Greek word for "bowed down" is *proskuneo*, which means "to worship, to kiss toward." No man worships another man...but he worships God.

**Matthew 9:18–26 (NIV)**

> A ruler came and knelt before Him and said, "My daughter has just died. But come and put your hand on her, and she will live" (v. 18).

Again, the ruler would not have worshiped a mere man.

**Mark 5:6 (KJV)**

> But when he saw Jesus afar off, he ran and worshiped him.

The demon-possessed man living in the tombs had a revelation that Christ was deity, the Son of God.

## AUTHORITY OVER SATAN

**Mark 3:14–15 (NIV)**

> He appointed twelve—designating them apostles—that they might be with him and that he might send them out to preach and to have authority to drive out demons.

If you follow Jesus, you are His disciple and you have this authority.

**Mark 6:7, 13**

> Calling the Twelve to him, he sent them out two by two and gave them authority over evil spirits....They drove out many demons and anointed many sick people with oil and healed them.

He gave them authority. As a result, they drove out demons and healed the sick.

**Mark 16:17–18**

Jesus said:

> These signs will accompany those who have believed: in My name they will cast out demons, they will speak with new tongues; they will pick up serpents, and if they drink any deadly poison, it will not hurt them; they will lay hands on the sick, and they will recover.

**Luke 10:19 (NIV)**

Jesus said to His disciples:

> I have given you authority to trample on snakes and scorpions and to overcome all the power of the enemy; nothing will harm you.

# MAN'S WISDOM VS. GOD'S WISDOM

### Isaiah 55:8–9 (NIV)

> For My thoughts are not your thoughts, neither are your ways My ways, declares the LORD. As the heavens are higher than the earth, so are My ways higher than your ways and My thoughts than your thoughts.

If God's thoughts, knowledge, and mind are that much greater than ours, why not seek His wisdom, rather than relying on man's? "It is better to take refuge in the LORD than to trust in man" (Ps. 118:8).

### 1 Corinthians 1:20 (NIV)

Paul wrote:

> Where is the wise man? Where is the scholar? Where is the philosopher of this age? Has not God made foolish the wisdom of the world?

### 1 Corinthians 1:23

Paul wrote:

> But we preach Christ crucified, to Jews a stumbling block and to Gentiles foolishness.

### 1 Corinthians 3:19–20 (AMP)

> For this world's wisdom is foolishness (absurdity and stupidity) with God...the Lord knows the thoughts and reasonings of the [humanly] wise and recognizes how futile they are.

# Appendix B

# MEDICAL DOCUMENTATION

I'M ALSO SHARING some medical reports, so you can see what my condition was, and what it is now.

In everything, I give glory to the Father who drew me to Himself, to the Son who loved me and gave Himself for me, and to the Holy Spirit, who filled me with God's love.

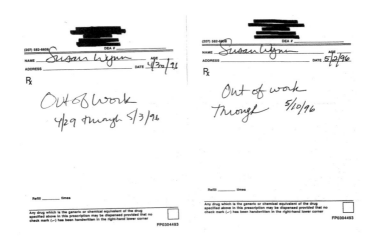

1996-04-30 and 1996-05-02: Out of Work Prescriptions

NAME ~~*Susan Wynn*~~

JUN 3 1996

ADDRESS _____ DATE _____

R

Mrs. Wynn is under my
care for a severe
head tremor.
She will not be able
to work until the tremor
is under better control.

Refill _____ times    PRN    NR    _____ M.D.

Any drug which is the generic or chemical equivalent of the drug specified
above in this prescription may be dispensed provided that the drug
dispensed is listed in the current edition of either the National Formulary or
the United States Pharmacopoeia and provided that no check mark ✓ has
been handwritten in the box inthe right-hand lower corner.

06/30/92                                    1401-K11218962

Given to ████████ on June 6, 1996
by ████████         @ 11:15 am.

1996-06-03: Out of Work Prescription

Patient: WYNN, SUSAN    MRN: ▓▓▓▓▓▓▓▓▓▓          Status: Signed
Author: ▓▓▓▓▓▓▓▓▓▓▓▓▓▓▓▓                         Visit Date: 01/22/98

Re: Susan Wynn          Brigham MR# ▓▓▓▓▓▓

Dear Dr. ▓▓▓▓▓▓

I just saw your patient, Susan Wynn, in our unit today. As you
are familiar with the history, Ibll only briefly summarize at
this time for my records.  The patient is a 42-year old woman
whose history began in 1986, when she had optic neuritis
associated with pain with eye movement in the right eye, with a
central scotoma lasting approximately three weeks, then went back
to normal.  A second attack was again in the right eye, in 1989,
which she described as kaleidoscopic vision with large letters
not completely seen.  Again, it lasted approximately one month,
but never totally resolved.  The next attack began in March of
1996, with optic neuritis on the left eye with a decrease in
vision and a þscarþ in the eye.  Her major problems began in
April of 1996, to August of 1996, when she developed a head
tremor which spread to her trunk and then developed into þrubral
tremorþ.  Multiple medications, well documented in your notes,
were tried, but nothing has seemed to help.  Although the tremor
has gotten somewhat better with five days of IV Solu-Medrol, it
has remained persistent to difficulty.  The patient started using
a cane in April of 1997, and has had gradual worsening of her
gait since that period.  The past two months, in particular,
sheþs had cramping, feet in a cast, and a more ataxic gait.  She
has been on Avonex since August of 1996, and though has not had
any clear attacks, has clearly continued to get worse.

The patient denies a history of diplopia or other neurologic
symptoms, though she did note a urinary difficulty with hesitancy
approximately six months ago.  Previous medical history is
remarkable for asthma, for which she is on medication.  Social
history is that both she and her husband are retired; her from
disability and he was in the military with an injury.  Family
history is unremarkable for autoimmune diseases.

1998-01-22: Letter from Brigham and Women's

*Medical Documentation*

Patient: WYNN,SUSAN  MRN: ▓▓▓▓▓
Author: ▓▓▓▓▓▓▓▓▓▓

Status: Signed
Visit Date:01/22/98

▓▓▓▓▓▓▓▓▓.
January 22, 1998
Page 2
          Re:  Susan Wynn
               #▓▓▓▓▓▓

A detailed exam was performed and documented in the enclosed Clinical Evaluation Form.  Ms. Wynn clearly has a rather severe head bobbing with an ataxic gait.  She has an EDSS of 6, AI of 2, and disease step of 3.  I reviewed the MRI, and there are only very few small lesions which are not very impressive on T2 weighted imaging.

Ms. Wynn appears to present someone who has not responded well to the interferons.  She is clearly losing function, and I would agree with using pulse Cyclophosphamide.  We could begin this here, and then continue up in Maine once she gets on a stable dose.  The general protocol that we use is pulse infusions with Solu-Medrol once every four weeks for a year, then every six weeks, 8 weeks, 10 weeks, 12 weeks, for a year.  The program generally lasts from 4 to 5 years.  I will try putting in a call to you today, hoping to just touch bases on Susan and some of the other patients you sent here.  Best personal regards.

Sincerely yours,



▓▓▓▓▓▓▓

▓▓▓

Enclosure: MS Clinical Evaluation Form

▓▓▓▓▓▓▓.

DD: 01/22/98
DT: 02/08/98
DV: 01/22/98
******** Approved but not reviewed by Attending Provider ********

1998-01-22: Letter from Brigham and Women's

PATIENT:  WYNN, SUSAN D.
 D.O.B.:  12/29/55
RECORD #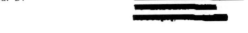
   DATE:  04/08/98

PROCEDURE: MRI BRAIN W GAD

HISTORY:  Patient has a history of possible demyelinating disease
with bilateral hand numbness and gait deterioration.

SCAN TECHNIQUE:  Sagittal T-1 and second echo T-2 weighted sequences
through the brain parenchyma were initially performed.  This was
followed by axial T-1 and second echo T-2 weighted sequences as well
as a FLAIR sequence through the brain parenchyma.  Gadolinium DTPA
was then given in the usual amount and the axial T-1 weighted
sequences were repeated.

SCAN FINDINGS:  Sagittal view shows one small high signal area
extending perpendicularly from the right lateral ventricle adjacent
to the corpus callosum. There may be a few small punctate high
signal areas also seen in the left parietal region and the right
parietal area.  No mass effect or midline shift is seen. The area
of the pons and brainstem area are relatively unremarkable.  Small
punctate areas of high signal are also seen in the bifrontal region
and a small single focus in the posterior superior thalamic area on
the left.  After injection of gadolinium DTPA, the axial images
were repeated.  Of note, no enhancing lesions or pathology within
the brain parenchyma could be defined.

IMPRESSION:  1.  A few small punctate areas of high signal are
                 seen near the left lateral ventricle in the
                 bifrontal region and posterior left thalamic
                 area all of which were present on the last study
                 and unchanged.  No new lesions are identified
                 or evidence of progression of disease. Differential
                 still remains either small areas of microvascular
                 disease or infarcts or possible small punctate
                 areas of demyelinization with no new lesions seen.
             2.  No enhancing lesions identified on the post
                 contrast studies.

─────────────────────────────
████████████████ M.D.

████
t: 04/09/98
cc:

1998-04-08: MRI Report

Patient: WYNN, SUSAN   MRN: ▮▮▮▮▮▮▮▮

Author: ▮▮▮▮▮▮▮▮▮▮▮▮▮▮

September 17, 1998

RE: Susan Wynn
▮▮▮▮▮▮▮▮

Dear Dr. ▮▮▮▮▮▮

I understand that Susan Wynn will be seeing you for a follow-up. She has a relapsing/remitting progressive form of multiple sclerosis, did not respond to the Interferon. When I saw her back in January 1998, she had an EDSS of 6, and an ambulation index of 2. We began monthly pulse cyclophosphamide, and though only recently got her up to what believe to be a therapeutic dose. She reports now that at approximately 5 months she started to feel a marked improvement, now has gone from walking 25 feet in approximately 7.5 seconds with a moderate degree of ataxia, to today she walked 25 feet in approximately 4.5 seconds with an almost normal gait. She continues, however, to have mild head bobbing slightly, though is better then when I last saw her. She is tolerating the cyclophosphamide well without much in the way of side effects.

Detailed exam was performed and documented on the enclosed Clinical Evaluation Form.

Susan is quite pleased, as am I, over her response to the therapy.

The plan is to continue the pulse cyclophosphamide at q. four week intervals for the next six months, then I will reevaluate her. If she continues to do well, we will begin a slow taper, increasing the time between the doses. She would also like to have the

1998-09-17: Letter from Brigham and Women's

Patient: WYNN, SUSAN   MRN:
Author: ███████████████████

Status: Signed
Visit Date:09/17/98

███████████████

Page Two
September 17, 1998

RE: Susan Wynn

██████████

therapy up in Maine, and I think this is a very good time to do
this. She will discuss this with you in detail, and whoever will
actually do the infusions can contact our,████████████████
████████████████████ and she can provide you with the
details of the protocol.

With my best regards.

Sincerely yours,


██████████████.


████████


Enc:  MS Clinical Evaluation Form

████████████████████


██████████████

██████████████
████████████

******** Not reviewed by Attending Physician ********

1998-09-17: Letter from Brigham and Women's

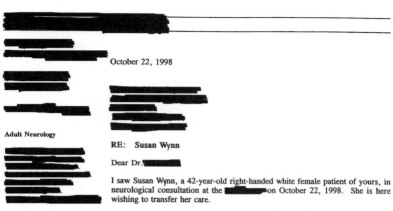

October 22, 1998

**Adult Neurology**

RE: Susan Wynn

Dear Dr.

I saw Susan Wynn, a 42-year-old right-handed white female patient of yours, in neurological consultation at the ▇▇▇▇ on October 22, 1998. She is here wishing to transfer her care.

**Pediatric & Adult Neurology**

In 1986, the patient had a bout of right-sided optic neuritis. She says she had another bout in 1989. In April 1996, the patient developed another bout of right optic neuritis which was documented by her eye doctor. Around that time, she began to develop an unusual head tremor as well. She was subsequently evaluated by ▇▇▇▇ in Augusta. Klonopin, Mysoline, and Tegretol were tried for the head tremor. The tremor increased and began to occur at the waist and then her right arm. She was told she had a rubral tremor. Due to lack of success with oral medicines, the patient was given a trial of IV methylprednisolone. Her symptoms of tremor resolved. This lasted 2-3 months. In January 1997, the patient began to develop leg buzzing and vibrating. She was started on Avonex in the summer of 1996 and then started cycle of 3 days of IV methylprednisolone monthly. In the late fall 1997, ▇▇▇▇ evaluated her and diagnosed her as having progressive multiple sclerosis. He recommended Cytoxan / methylprednisolone combination therapy. She has been on that for about 5 months and feels as though she has started to improve.

**Diagnostic Services**

Electromyography

Electroencephalography
Ambulatory EEG

Evoked Potentials
Electronystagmography

Cranial Ultrasound
Transcranial Doppler
Carotid Doppler

The patient has had 5 MRIs that I was provided a record of. Most of them were negative, although the last couple have shown some white matter signal abnormalities. The cerebrospinal fluid was negative on 2 occasions: May 1996 and January 1998. Auditory, posterior tibial somatosensory evoked potentials and visual evoked potentials were negative.

I have reviewed voluminous notes which are in the patient's chart.

Recently, the patient has been getting 2,700 mg. of IV cyclophosphamide monthly with IV methylprednisolone and Zofran.

**Past Medical History:** As above.

**Current Medications:** See list in patient's chart. Currently, she is taking:
Flovent
Maxair

Page 2
October 22, 1998
**Susan Wynn**

Claritin
Vancenase
Erythromycin around dental work
Cytoxan
Neurontin
PremPro
Methylprednisolone
Torecan
Zanaflex
Zofran
Prilosec
Gaviscon
Tums
Vitamin C
Vitamin E
Multiple vitamin
Current Neurontin dose: 400 mg. b.i.d.

**Social History:**
Retired
Married
Used to be a computer specialist at Togus.

**Neurologic Evaluation:** Disclosed a well developed, well nourished woman, accompanied by her husband. Cranial nerve exam shows 20/20 visual acuity on both sides. Visual fields were full to finger counting. Pupils were symmetric at 5 mm. and both showed 2+ reaction to light without afferent pupillary defect. She has mild optic atrophy on the left. Lids, ocular motility, facial sensation, facial symmetry, muscles of mastication, hearing, tongue, palate, and shoulder shrug are normal. Motor examination shows a wide-based ataxic gait with right leg weaker than left. There is no pronator drift. Muscle bulk is normal. Tone is increased in both lower extremities. Cerebellar tests were normal. The patient has an affirmative tremor of the head which fluctuates in intensity during the examination and seems to diminish somewhat with distraction. Sensory exam was normal. Tendon reflexes were 2+ right biceps and radialis jerks and 3+ at all other stations in the upper and lower extremities. Toes are down-going.

**Impression:** ? Primary progressive multiple sclerosis versus secondary progressive multiple sclerosis.

**Recommendations:** I will speak with Dr. ███████ office and evaluate for the type of regimen that she is on. She wishes to transfer the treatment to ██████ and that seems reasonable to me. I will plan to see her in follow up after 6 weeks. Thank you for allowing me to participate in your patient's care.

Sincerely yours,

cc:

Dictated but not read

1998-10-22: Neurologist to Family Physician

90

**NEUROLOGIC RE-EVALUATION**

*BEFORE*

NAME: ~~Susan Wynn~~  REF. PHYS.: ████████  DATE: *10 25 99*  DOB: *12-29 55*

HISTORY: ___ — SEE LETTER.

LOTS OF FATIGUE — MUSCLE FATIGUE
AND ALSO THRU THE DAY — GEN.

HA — CONSTANT DAILY HA — VERTEX — RETRO-ORB
AND FEELS BETTER W/ DOWNWARD PRESSURE ON
HEAD.

EPISODE OF WEAKNESS / START OF FATIGUE 9/1/99
SEEMS DISCRETE ONSET.

OBJECTIVE:

MULTIPLE RED INJ. SITES.

MEDICATIONS:

AMANTADINE 100 +ID

ASSESSMENT/PLAN:

MS EXACERBATION

$\overline{5}$
TREMOR — ↑ NEURONTIN TO 700 QID.
FATIGUE —
     TRY TX IVMP — IF NOT BETTER
     IF NOT → PROZAC, RITALIN

FOLLOW UP IN: *3 wks* / or prn problems.      ~~PEL~~

**Thank you.**

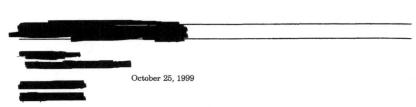

October 25, 1999

**Adult Neurology**

RE: Susan Wynn

Dear ████████,

I saw Susan Wynn in extensive follow-up on October 25, 1999, regarding her MS. She presented me with a letter outlining her current problems.

She had an episode of weakness in the lower extremities and severe fatigue which started in early September 1999. There seems to have been a discrete onset of these symptoms. She has continued to suffer with leg weakness. She also complains of constant daily headache and increasing fatigue.

**Examination:** On examination today she shows an EDSS score of 3.5. Functional system scores were pyramidal 3, cerebellar 3, bowel and bladder 1, visual 0, brain stem 0, sensory 0, cerebral 1, and other 1, with EDSS of 3.5. Her gait and nine-hole peg test were not substantially changed.

**Pediatric & Adult Neurology**

**Impression:**
1. MS exacerbation September 1, 1999, with corticospinal tract dysfunction.
2. Severe tremor.
3. Severe fatigue.

**Diagnostic Services**

Electromyography
Nerve Conduction Studies

Electroencephalography
Ambulatory EEG

Evoked Potentials
Electronystagmography

Cranial Ultrasound
Transcranial Doppler
Carotid Doppler

**Recommendations:**
1. Trial of IV Methylprednisolone x3 days.
2. Increase Neurontin to 700 mg q.i.d. regarding tremor.
3. Follow-up in approximately three weeks. If she doesn't seem to be responding as far as her severe fatigue is concerned, then Prozac or Ritalin may be added.

Thank you for allowing me to participate in your patient's care.

Sincerely,

Dictated but not read

1999-10-25: Neurologist to Family Physician

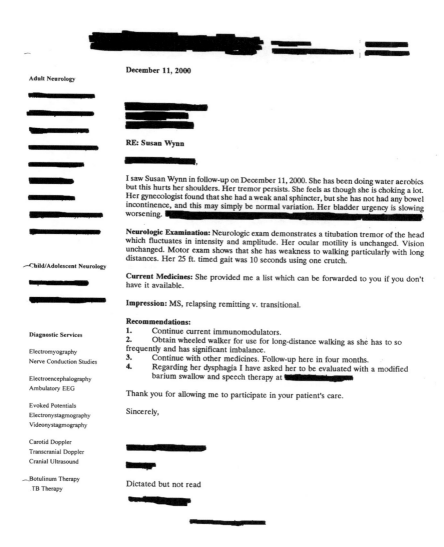

**December 11, 2000**

**Adult Neurology**

**RE: Susan Wynn**

I saw Susan Wynn in follow-up on December 11, 2000. She has been doing water aerobics but this hurts her shoulders. Her tremor persists. She feels as though she is choking a lot. Her gynecologist found that she had a weak anal sphincter, but she has not had any bowel incontinence, and this may simply be normal variation. Her bladder urgency is slowing worsening.

**Neurologic Examination:** Neurologic exam demonstrates a titubation tremor of the head which fluctuates in intensity and amplitude. Her ocular motility is unchanged. Vision unchanged. Motor exam shows that she has weakness to walking particularly with long distances. Her 25 ft. timed gait was 10 seconds using one crutch.

**Current Medicines:** She provided me a list which can be forwarded to you if you don't have it available.

**Impression:** MS, relapsing remitting v. transitional.

**Recommendations:**
1.  Continue current immunomodulators.
2.  Obtain wheeled walker for use for long-distance walking as she has to so frequently and has significant imbalance.
3.  Continue with other medicines. Follow-up here in four months.
4.  Regarding her dysphagia I have asked her to be evaluated with a modified barium swallow and speech therapy at

Thank you for allowing me to participate in your patient's care.

Sincerely,

Dictated but not read

*Child/Adolescent Neurology*

**Diagnostic Services**

Electromyography
Nerve Conduction Studies

Electroencephalography
Ambulatory EEG

Evoked Potentials
Electronystagmography
Videonystagmography

Carotid Doppler
Transcranial Doppler
Cranial Ultrasound

Botulinum Therapy
TB Therapy

2000-12-11: Neurologist to Internal Medicine Physician

**Adult Neurology**

October 17, 2001

Neurologic Reevaluation

*Re:   Susan Wynn*

Susan Wynn was seen in reevaluation on October 17, 2001. She says that her hands are "killing her." She is getting a lot of zinging and tingling sensations in both hands. It is similar to the sensation that occurs when your hands are "frozen and start warming up." She got some resolution of pain with amitriptyline. Right and left hands are equally affected. She is now getting more persistent numbness and tingling.

Regarding her MS she feels rather well.

**Nerve Conduction Studies:** See NCS worksheet.
1.  **Right median motor nerve conduction study** shows prolonged distal motor latency at 4.8 milliseconds with normal findings otherwise.
2.  **Right median F-wave** normal.
3.  **Left median motor nerve conduction study** shows prolonged distal motor latency at 4.8 milliseconds with normal findings otherwise.
4.  **Right ulnar motor nerve conduction study** normal.
5.  **Right ulnar F-wave** normal.
6.  **Right median sensory nerve conduction study shows** prolonged distal sensory latency at 3.1 milliseconds with moderate reduction in SNAP amplitude.
7.  **Left median sensory nerve conduction study shows** prolonged distal sensory latency at 3.3 milliseconds with moderate reduction in SNAP amplitude.
8.  **Right ulnar sensory nerve conduction study** normal.

**EMG:** Not performed.

**Impression:** Bilateral carpal tunnel syndrome, moderate. Findings are worse than when compared with the previous study.

**Recommendations:** In view of the above findings, continued nighttime splints are indicated, however, if there is a persistent failure to respond carpal tunnel release may be indicated. The patient will get back to me to let me know her decision about that.

**~Child/Adolescent Neurology**

**Diagnostic Services**

Electromyography
Nerve Conduction Studies

Electroencephalography
Ambulatory EEG

Evoked Potentials
Electronystagmography
Videonystagmography

Carotid Doppler
Transcranial Doppler
Cranial Ultrasound

~Botulinum Therapy
.TB Therapy

2001-10-17: Neurologic Re-Evaluation

AFTER

▮▮▮▮▮▮▮▮▮▮▮▮▮▮

Name Susan Wynn   Ref Phys ▮▮▮▮▮ Date 4/16/02 DOB 6/29/55

**History:**

THRU HER CHURCH (GARDINER FREE METHODIST)
SHE'S BEEN HEALED.

• HER MS IS HEALED.

• HER CTS SX CLEARED.

• GOING INTO ORDINATION PROGRAM — PLANNING
TO START THAT IN SEPT.

• HAS GIVEN SERMONS, TESTIMONIALS, ETC —
MOST RECENTLY IN SCHROON LAKE, NY.

| Meds listed by pt: |
|---|
|  |
|  |
|  |
|  |
|  |
|  |
|  |
|  |

**Interim medical hx:**

EOMN.

**Exam:** see reverse for detail

VIBR (N)   Exam - NML

**Impressions:**

? MS

**Reviewed with patient:**
☐ MRI/Xray films ☐ Other _____
☐ Lab _____

**Plan:**

**Time spent with patient:** _____ min.
☐ counseling
☐ med discussion
☐ family conf w/ ☐ spouse ☐ parent ☐ child

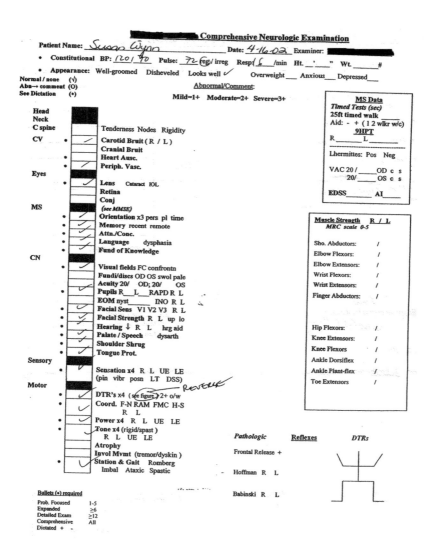

2002-04-16: Comprehensive Neurologic Exam

| Name, first name | WYNN SUSAN | Eye/Pupil | Left eye (OS) / 5.0 |
| ID |  | Date/Time | 10.15.2008 / 05:20 p.m. |
| Date of birth | 12.29.1955 | Test duration | 02:06 |
| Gender | female | Program/Strategy | G1 / TOP |
| Refraction S/C/A | / / | # Stages/Phases | 4 / 1 |
| Acuity |  | Method | Standard / White/White |
| IOP |  | Stimulus/Duration | III / 100 |
| Notes |  | Background [cd/m2] | 10 |
|  |  | # Questions/Repetitions | 69 / 0 |
|  |  | # Catch trials | pos 1 / 3, neg 0 / 4 |

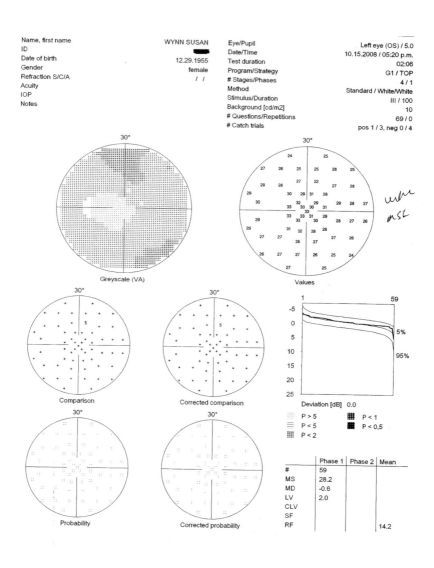

|  | Phase 1 | Phase 2 | Mean |
|---|---|---|---|
| # | 59 |  |  |
| MS | 28.2 |  |  |
| MD | -0.6 |  |  |
| LV | 2.0 |  |  |
| CLV |  |  |  |
| SF |  |  |  |
| RF |  |  | 14.2 |

2008-10-15: Field of Vision Exam Left Eye

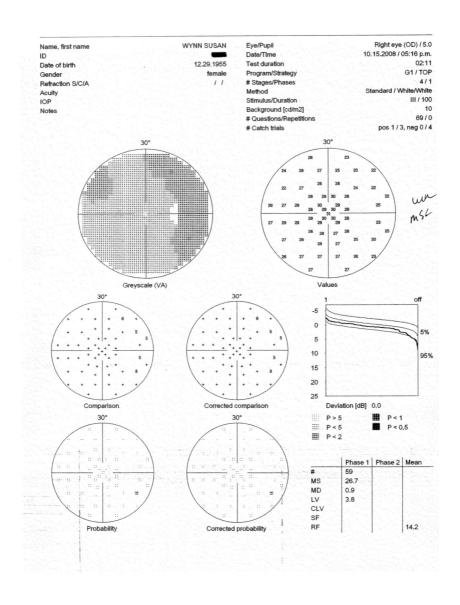

| Name, first name | WYNN SUSAN | Eye/Pupil | Right eye (OD) / 5.0 |
| ID | ▬ | Date/Time | 10.15.2008 / 05:16 p.m. |
| Date of birth | 12.29.1955 | Test duration | 02:11 |
| Gender | female | Program/Strategy | G1 / TOP |
| Refraction S/C/A | / / | # Stages/Phases | 4 / 1 |
| Acuity | | Method | Standard / White/White |
| IOP | | Stimulus/Duration | III / 100 |
| Notes | | Background [cd/m2] | 10 |
| | | # Questions/Repetitions | 69 / 0 |
| | | # Catch trials | pos 1 / 3, neg 0 / 4 |

Greyscale (VA)

Values

Comparison

Corrected comparison

Deviation [dB]   0.0

Probability

Corrected probability

P > 5      P < 1
P < 5      P < 0,5
P < 2

| | Phase 1 | Phase 2 | Mean |
|---|---|---|---|
| # | 59 | | |
| MS | 26.7 | | |
| MD | 0.9 | | |
| LV | 3.8 | | |
| CLV | | | |
| SF | | | |
| RF | | | 14.2 |

2008-10-15: Field of Vision Exam Right Eye

# ABOUT THE AUTHOR

R EV. SUE SAYS her life really began when she met Jesus
Christ. A graduate of the University of Maine, she enjoyed
a successful business career before MS shattered her life in
1996. Jesus Christ stepped in five years later and healed her.

After her healing, Sue received a strong word from the Lord
that she wasn't to return to her former career. Poetry soon began
to flow, and then lyrics and melodies. Her pastor advised her to
pursue ordination after he asked her to preach. The Free Methodist
Church ordained Sue in 2007 and her husband, Jeff, the following
year.

Called to Florida in 2009, Sue and her husband Jeff began Set
Free Ministries. They proclaim Jesus Christ to the world, ministering healing and restoration to whomever they meet.

# CONTACT THE AUTHOR

## E-mail:

SWYNN123@AOL.COM

## Website:

WWW.SUSANWYNNWORDS.COM

## Facebook:

## Set Free Ministries

## Blog:

## Fromdeathtolife.wordpress.com